WHEN THE
MUSIC CHANGES

God bless you along your journey!

Elfreda Massie
5-20-18

ELFREDA WINSTEAD MASSIE, PhD

PLATFORM

PRESS

Bucks County
Pennsylvania

I know God will not give me
anything I can't handle.
I just wish that He didn't
trust me so much.

—Mother Teresa

Editorial, production, and publishing services provided by
Platform Press
Winans Kuenstler Publishing, LLC
93 East Court Street
Doylestown, Pennsylvania 18901
(215) 500-1989
www.WKPublishing.com

Printed in the United States

ISBN: 978-0-9974930-2-3

1 2 3 4 5 6 7 8 9 0
First Paperback Edition

Table of Contents

Dedication

This book was written to demonstrate my relationship with God. God is truth. God is mercy. God is grace. God is Love. It was written to demonstrate my relationship with my family, whose love and support are unending. It was written to demonstrate my belief in myself that I am an overcomer and nothing is too hard for God and me to handle.

"There are three things that will endure—faith, hope, and love—and the greatest of these is love." - 1 Corinthians 13:13

Since birth, my journey has enabled me to experience the frivolity of childhood, the value and success that come from hard work, worldly happiness, professional success, the pain of disappointment, the injury of frustration, and a multitude of life's daily experiences. However, God has been the template and foundation upon which I lived. His love and support helped me understand and appreciate the true love and support I received from family and special friends.

This book is dedicated to my Daddy, God's gift of true manhood, patience, and love.

In the words of my brother, this book is also dedicated "to all the ancestors who believed in the improbable and worked toward the possible ... all those who gave their lives for generations born and unborn to have a better life ... those who nurtured, supported, and believed in me," even before I was born.

"I knew you before I formed you in your mother's womb. Before you were born I set you apart and appointed you as my spokesman to the world." - Jeremiah 1:5

Some of you are reading this book because you understand the battle and the victory, the pain and the joy, and the blessings of perseverance and waiting for small miracles. I trust that my experiences may provide direction, solitude, and peace.

Acknowledgments

I can hardly believe that this book has finally been completed. Throughout the writing process there have been many obstacles and distractions, but thanks to a faithful God, the perseverance of my editor and his assistant, the love of my family, and the support of my friends, I present you with a glimpse of my life. Through this book you will see how faith, family, and friends have sustained me.

With gratitude and humility, I thank:

Foster Winans, for your patience for truly listening and encouraging me to get this book finished; for taking the time to walk in my shoes and in my world; for being a great thought partner and editor; and for your honesty. Had you not shared your story and your pain, I may not have taken this journey. There is a greater reason that our paths have crossed.

Raquel Pidal, for your kind nature and your work behind the scenes; for the many hours you labored on this book.

Dr. Kofi Boahene, for saving my face and giving me back my life; for that big smile just when I needed it; and for being a living example of the Good Samaritan.

Anil Bhave, for never giving up on my knee or me; for giving me back mobility.

DeeDee, for just being you.

This book could not have been written without the love and support of my family:

Thanks to my husband, Leonard, for lovingly contributing to each chapter of my life and for nudging me by repeatedly asking, "Have you finished the book yet?"

Thanks to my daughters, Nicole and Michelle, for your example of what it means to be strong women of God; for your love and laughter; and for carrying on the legacy.

Thanks to my granddaughters, Kadence, Anaya, Addison, and Josephine, for bringing me unspeakable joy.

Thanks to my mother, Barbara Jean Winstead Mills, for your unconditional love and unwavering support.

Thanks to Wheeler, Mary, and Debby, for being the best brother and sisters and for encouraging me through the ups and downs of my life.

Last but not least, thank *you* for spending time with this book. May my story inspire you to find the blessings in your life and the comfort in your faith.

Introduction

Why do some people experience more than their share of hardship yet manage to remain positive and flourish while others who have enjoyed good health, stable families, and relative privilege stumble over the slightest bump in the road?

The question has intrigued me as someone who has experienced a generous helping of hardship. It's a question that I've contemplated in my roles as a public educator, community leader, woman of faith, spouse, and mother. It's a question that has special relevance to me as an African American who has wondered, as many do, why some children who grow up in modest circumstances in notorious neighborhoods succeed where so many seem to falter.

Is the determination it takes to rise above our challenges a function of nature, baked in at birth? Are some people genetically predisposed to confront and challenge adversity and negativity? Or is it nurture? What role do we as parents, educators, and community leaders play in helping or hindering the ability of others to meet and rise above life's obstacles?

The book you hold in your hands is my answer. Yours may differ, but it's likely you will find some universal truths here that could help you help yourself through hard times and influence the ability of others to do the same. On my unscientific journey of discovery, I have examined my experiences and reactions for clues to how I prevailed in the face of virulent racism and multiple health crises, as well as all the other stressors everyone faces in their families, work, and around money.

My hypothesis was simple: if we can decode why some people prevail in spite of their sorrows, maybe we can do a better job of preparing our children to face them and supporting our family, friends, and colleagues through them. Where do winning life skills come from and how can we nurture them?

My conclusion is that what sustains me—what has allowed me to honestly say I have led a rich, rewarding, and joyful life in spite of it all—is the power I draw from my self-identity. What that means is more complicated than it sounds. It's not about race, but it is about culture. It's not about religion, but it is about faith. It's not about gender, but it is about tradition. It's not about pride, but it is about dignity.

My identity—my self-perception—is a jigsaw puzzle that includes every aspect of my upbringing and life experience. It has been shaped by the knowledge that the people in my life who mattered most were praying for me before I was even born; by the fact I was the eldest daughter; by family history as passed on by my elders; by culture, community, and spiritual beliefs and rituals, including my faith in God; and by the people with whom I chose to share my life and those who entrusted me with their friendship and love.

I realized that the most important elements of my

identity were the result of an abundance of adversity. I sometimes feel that I have, as Zora Neale Hurston once wrote, "been in Sorrow's kitchen and licked out all the pots." I excelled as a student in spite of deliberate efforts to deny me opportunities because of my race. I learned to hold my head high as a youngster in the face of the shocking and sometimes violent behavior of others.

I believe I became a better wife because I nearly lost my husband in a car accident on our honeymoon. I became a better mother and a more compassionate person because I nearly lost the use of my legs in that accident. I became a better educator because of the discrimination I encountered in the workplace. My faith made me a stronger and more compassionate person, able to weather all sorts of sorrows.

My character has been defined more by trial than by triumph, and with purpose rather than by accident. I have at times felt broken figuratively as well as literally. With purpose, I began writing this book as catharsis and as a possible beacon of hope for others who, like many I have met, need one.

A major inspiration for this book was another book, *The Blessedness of Brokenness*, by Pastor Matthew Barnett. Published in 2012, it is a collection of stories of people whose faith helped them face adversity and thrive. Barnett makes the case that every setback is an opportunity to shape oneself to be more like God. He wrote that, "The brokenness in your life is not your enemy but a friend you just haven't met."

A book with a similar theme and title, *The Blessings of Brokenness*, had been published fifteen years earlier. Author Charles F. Stanley, senior pastor of First Baptist Church in Atlanta, wrote that, "After brokenness, we can experience God's greatest blessings. The dawn after a very dark and storm-wracked night is glorious. Joy after a period of intense mourning can be ecstatic."

I encountered Barnett's book at a low point in my life, after being diagnosed with a debilitating medical condition that interfered with my eyesight and contributed to my losing a valued and hard-won professional career. I was devastated, so the stories of others who had been devastated held a powerful appeal. My faith is important to me and I could relate.

But I wondered if there was more to the blessedness of brokenness than faith and prayer alone. After all, it wasn't prayer that gave me the courage as a seven-year-old to defy a teacher who paddled me for no good reason. My courage came from my identity as the granddaughter of a woman who was a respected leader in our community, someone who never hesitated to speak out against injustice.

It wasn't prayer alone that got me back on my feet after the car accident when the doctors said I'd never walk normally again. It was my identity as a member of a family of people who refused to be seen as victims, a descendant of South Carolina slaves and sharecroppers who fought to educate their children and refused to accept things the way they were. That identity gave me such determination that, against two-to-one odds, I found a doctor who could help me do it.

All the parts of the puzzle of my identity give me the dignity to persevere and to find the sweetness in my sorrows, the blessings in my brokenness, the lessons in my losses. When I became ill and needed major surgery to remove a rare tumor in my brain, I kept my complaints to myself, so much so that I alarmed my family by withholding the fact that I was having Alzheimer-like symptoms.

My self-identity as a fighter and survivor would not let me surrender to victimhood.

I prayed for help, guidance, and strength, but I also did the research to find the best doctor available to me, one who had just invented a revolutionary procedure that made the necessary surgery safer and less intrusive. Before I let him perform the procedure, we discussed the role of faith in healing and I was assured that we shared a belief in God's power to heal. You should pray for a good doctor, but you better also pray for a doctor who's going to be praying for you.

My siblings and I grew up hearing a consistent message from our elders about what was expected of us when faced with a crisis, a disappointment, or a sorrow. We heard certain favorite Bible verses again and again: "And we know that all things work together for good to them that love God, to them who are the called according to his purpose."*

When I had children of my own, I passed some of these scriptures on in my own words. "No matter how deep the hurt, you can take one day to cry. Then pull yourself together, get up, and keep moving forward. God allows us to go through difficult times, but He never leaves us."

My husband, Leonard, pastor of our church, often says in his sermons that, "Our present circumstances are not our conclusion."

My experiences have convinced me that we parents, educators, religious, and community leaders can make a difference in how children feel about their identity and, in doing so, teach them skills that will help them find strength and dignity in their sorrows and suffering.

None of this is simple or easy. Nor can it be expressed

---

* Romans 8:28, King James Version

as a formula or a set of hard and fast rules. But as you'll read in the pages ahead, how we define ourselves is ultimately up to each of us and that self-definition can be the crucial element that determines how well we cope with life's inevitable sorrows.

With modesty and humility—not as an expert, but as an expert witness—I invite you to join me on this journey with the hope that you will find some inspiration that— at the limits of your grief, disappointment, or pain—will help you find the dignity to overcome your adversities.

Elfreda Winstead Massie, PhD
Bowie, MD 2016

WHEN THE
MUSIC CHANGES

Part I
The Power of
Family Mythology

One:

When The Music Changes

*L*eonard and I were on our way home from our honeymoon in the Pocono Mountains of eastern Pennsylvania in April 1972 when it happened—when our troubles began. That dark snowy night, one of us would be pronounced dead and the other would be presumed crippled for life.

Leonard was a college man, a senior at the University of Maryland, and I, who had already gotten my degree, was teaching in an elementary school in Baltimore County. We had grown up as neighbors in a development of two-story frame row houses originally called Monongahela Heights. It had been built in a suburb of Pittsburgh to house steel and rubber workers needed to build the machinery of victory during World War II.

When I was a child, one side of the community was black and the other was white, with a playground in between. Although it was segregated, the men worked together in the steel plants and their kids played together in the common playground. As I grew up, the white families steadily moved out until the 300 or so housing units were almost all occupied by black families. It had been renamed the Whitaker Projects, after the family that first settled the area. As teenagers, we nicknamed it "The Jects."

As low-income housing, the Whitaker Projects had a unique history and features. It had been designed for the US Army during World War II by a world-famous architect, Edward Durell Stone. Stone had designed Radio City Music Hall and dozens of luxury homes for people like the Rockefellers. When the war broke out, he had enlisted and, in addition to designing Monongahela Heights, was in charge of building Army Air Force bases.

Unlike towering inner-city projects, ours was laid out in clusters of two-story row homes that felt like mini-neighborhoods on a wooded hillside overlooking the Monongahela River. The clusters were separated by patches of open space, and the neighborhood was insulated from the rest of the town by a single entrance that led to a looping roadway—Midway Drive, named for the Pacific island of World War II fame.

Whitaker was in every sense a community unto itself, both by geography and, when I was a child, by culture. If a neighbor spotted you engaging in some mischief, you could count on your mother or father knowing about it by the time you got home and you could expect an appropriate punishment.

Some of my favorite memories are of my grandmother, the woman who most influenced my worldview. In my eyes and in those of the many people she stood up for, Estelle Martin Cartledge—my friends and I called her Nina—was the Rosa Parks or the Harriet Tubman of Whitaker. She was outspoken but with a graciousness that won people over in spite of themselves.

When we grandchildren got old enough to get our drivers' licenses, we became her chauffeurs. She made frequent trips to do her food shopping and was always visiting a shut-in or dropping off some of her famous homemade bread rolls. One day the counter clerk at the butcher shop made the mistake of trying to pass off a cheaper cut of meat than the one she'd requested.

"Now you just wait a minute! That's not right! You're not going to do that to me, and you're not going to do it to anyone." In unison, the heads of the white customers snapped to attention. The clerk froze with a stricken look.

"You're not going to put this kind of meat out for colored people. You go right back and get that butcher and I'll show him the piece I want."

"Yes, ma'am! Yes, Miss Cartledge. You're right, Miss Cartledge!"

Sometimes when she got her dander up, she'd start quoting scripture, calling on God and, depending on the circumstances, trying to pray the Hell out of you. Sometimes she'd enlist folks from the church to come and pray with her.

She had a scripture for every situation. She prayed about and for everybody, whether you wanted prayer or not. She was always taking care of somebody, feeding the hungry, looking after the infirm. I grew up knowing her as a fierce aproned role model in shining armor.

That keen awareness about right and wrong, about standing up for yourself and for others, I learned first-hand when I was in second grade, one of the few black children in a mostly white elementary school, Lowell, that was almost a mile down the hill from home.

7

My seat was next to a white girl, Marcia, with whom I'd become friends. Our fathers worked together at US Steel in Duquesne, Pennsylvania. When my father was in an accident and couldn't drive to work, her father came to our segregated neighborhood to pick him up each day.

I wore my hair in those days with bangs in front and the rest in braids. One day I became so curious about the texture of her hair and asked if I could comb it for her. She said yes, so I combed her hair. Then she wanted to comb mine. We were just kids who'd finished our assignment and were having fun in class.

Suddenly the teacher loomed over us. She snatched the comb out of my hand and scolded the other girl.

"Don't you ever put your comb in a colored person's hair!" Then she paddled me.

I started crying. Through my sobs I said, "I'm gonna tell my grandma!" I pulled away and she snapped, "You're going to sit down!"

I sat there snuffling, humiliated, and gathering up my courage. We kids were never allowed to defy a teacher, and to walk home in the middle of a school day was unheard of. But I knew I didn't deserve that paddling. After fuming for a few minutes, I just stood up and walked out of the room as fast as I could, the teacher shouting, "You get back here, right now!"

I stormed out the doors and ran most of the way up the street, down a long, steep hill, past the church, straight to my grandmother's house, and burst in the door.

"What in the world, chile? Baby, why aren't you in school?"

"The teacher paddled me for no good reason." I explained with pint-sized indignity what had happened.

When I finished she arched a brow.

"Nothing else? That's what happened?"

I was a good student. I loved school. I paid attention and I never did the sorts of things that deserved paddling.

"Yes. That's all."

She drew herself up, eyes flashing. "You just wait a minute while I put on my hat."

She got her purse, put on her good skirt and lipstick, pinned on her hat, took my hand, and we marched back down the hill to school. I was so proud of her! I looked forward to seeing the expressions on the faces of the children and the teacher when we got there. Someone was in trouble and it wasn't me!

When my grandmother flung open the front door, the building seemed to tremble and the air crackle. I followed as she walked straight into my classroom. She told me to go sit in my chair, turned to the teacher, and, in a steely but polite tone, said, "Come here outside in the hallway. I want to talk to you."

I can only imagine what she said. All I know is the teacher apologized to me and I never got paddled for anything ever again. This was a defining experience, an epic anecdote that I have returned to time and again for validation and strength in the face of adversity.

My grandmother's influence wove itself throughout my childhood and played a role in my marriage to Leonard. It began the day he had a run-in with her when he was about twelve. She kept a garden and nurtured a few peach trees. One hot summer day my future husband and his best friend, Gregory, helped themselves to a few peaches.

Although we kids sometimes thought she had eyes in the back of her head, my grandmother didn't need them. She *was* the eyes, ears, and the conscience of Whitaker. Nothing much escaped her attention and when she caught the boys red-handed, her stern-yet-spiritual form of justice swiftly followed—every Saturday for the rest of the summer they would clean the church in preparation for Sunday services.

Like so many African American communities, the beating heart of Mon Heights was a house of worship. Ours was Morning Star Baptist Church, up the hill from the Jects. It is a small church, as churches go, tucked into a hillside in a residential neighborhood. Its role in my family, however, was huge.

My great-grandfather on my mother's side, Rev. Peter Paris Martin, was a Baptist minister in McCormick, South Carolina, when the younger members of his family moved away to the Pittsburgh area. He helped them plan and organize a new church in West Mifflin. The church got its name one morning when two of the ministers involved were out walking, noticed a morning star, and took it as a sign.

All but three of the first members of Morning Star Baptist were my relatives. Two uncles were its first deacons. My mother, Barbara Jean Cartledge, was the first to be baptized there and my Aunt Stella Mae was the first to be married there.

My grandmother and her sister, my Aunt Mae, would go around the neighborhood on Sunday mornings, round up the children, and shepherd them to Sunday School. There were Bible verses to learn but the church also entered the youngsters in area spelling competitions.

My grandmother was the matriarch of our family and a church leader. We grandkids were her little Hebrew slaves, obliged to answer her call whenever there were chores to be done, a church supper to be served, and then dishes to be washed. We were expected to always be the first to arrive on Sundays and the last to leave, after sweeping and gathering up things people had left on the pews. If the church doors were open, we Winstead kids—my brother Wheeler, my sisters Mary and Debby, and myself—were there.

On Saturdays my sisters and I, along with all the young girls, had choir practice. That's what we were doing when Leonard and Gregory showed up to begin serving their sentences.

We were all about twelve years old and they liked the math—two boys and all those girls. After the first Saturday, they eagerly looked forward to the next. They listened to us sing and then one Sunday Gregory joined in. He happened to have a beautiful voice so my grandmother changed his chore to singing. "Leonard, you just keep sweeping."

I'd known Leonard long before then as just a boy in the neighborhood. He had the paper route in the Jects for awhile and lived next door to us for a time, but I paid him no particular attention. He was a bit of a bookworm and an introvert. I was a bit of a tomboy and very social.

One Saturday Leonard suddenly announced to my grandmother, "Miss Cartledge, I'm going to marry your granddaughter when I grow up."

My grandmother was very patient with everyone, no matter what sort of nonsense a person might say to her. This child declaring his love must have been sweet, innocent, and amusing.

"Oh, really? Now, why do you think you're going to marry my granddaughter?"

"I just like her! And she sings in the choir, and she's just really nice, and I think she's pretty."

My grandmother reported all this to me and I laughed it off. "Oh, please!"

"Well, you know, Elfreda, he seems like a nice little Christian boy."

I just rolled my eyes. Another reason to dismiss him!

If Leonard paid attention to any other girls, I never noticed. Although he became the star and the captain of his sports teams, he was a loner who hung out with his one best friend. I loved to dance and my sisters and I used to win contests. Leonard didn't know how to dance. He didn't go bowling or skating.

Even if Leonard had been cool, I preferred to hang out with friends who were a few years older than me, guys who already had their first cars. Leonard was no competition.

Nevertheless, by the time we were in junior high he started telling everybody he was going to marry me. Boys I was dating would ask, "What's with this Leonard?"

"Ignore him. He doesn't know what he's talking about. I don't know why he says that." Leonard was complicating my social life and I didn't like it one bit.

I told him, "Leonard, that's crazy! I could never marry you. You're like a brother."

By the time I capitulated, we'd become best friends and I realized it wasn't such a bad idea to marry your best friend. He'd worked during high school, making good money, and then got a scholarship to attend the University of Maryland where they'd lined him up with a construction job paying union wages.

When we'd become an item he bought me a fur coat and himself a nice used car with fancy wheel covers. My mother was somewhat scandalized by such extravagance but no one was surprised when we announced our engagement. We drove off on our honeymoon in our big tinted glasses, Afros, and flapping bell-bottoms.

That day, the day we were going home to begin our lives as husband and wife, an inch or two of snow had fallen in the mountains. By the time we were packed and began the long drive to Pittsburgh, the pavement had become as slick as a dinner plate. We were going down a hill when Leonard realized he wasn't going to be able to make the next bend. He stood on the brakes. They locked and the car skidded toward a massive tree, slamming into it on the driver's side. Then we hit something else, the passenger door flew open, and I was airborne.

What happened in the next minutes, before help arrived, is mostly lost to me in the fog of the moment and the time that's passed. We were in the middle of nowhere, in a mountainous resort area, out of season. In the distance some dogs were barking frantically. I couldn't feel any sensation in my legs. Were they cut off?

"Jesus save me!" I prayed aloud. "Jesus save me! Please don't let me die."

After what seemed liked a long time, a woman's voice replied, "We're not going to let you die."

It was a retired couple who lived in the nearest house. I had landed in a pasture where there were some bulls that were startled and began bellowing. That set the couple's dogs to barking, which alerted them.

Finally an ambulance rolled up, filling the dark night with its harsh flashing lights. When the attendants got to me I asked, "Where's Leonard? Where's my husband?"

"We didn't see anyone else," one said.

"He was driving. He has to be there."

They found Leonard in a ditch, and as I was being carried to the ambulance I could see in the glare a white sheet draped over a body on the roadway. No one had to explain it. Leonard was dead.

My next memory is being in an ambulance that was following the ambulance that had taken Leonard away. I didn't know it yet but both of my legs were badly broken, my left kneecap was shattered, and the muscles and tendons in both legs had been torn. The pain was excruciating.

Then we were each on a gurney in the hallway of a hospital emergency room. Leonard was alive! But his face was covered with blood and sticking out of his face and scalp were shards of glass. He'd been knocked out and cut up going through the windshield.

No one was tending to us. We watched as other people waiting for care—people with the flu, people with abdominal pain, and so on—went ahead of us. Nobody told us why they weren't treating us, but they didn't have to. If I could have summoned the strength I learned from my grandmother, I would have made a fuss, but I was in shock and too much pain.

Finally someone from the staff at the resort we'd just checked out of showed up. They had called our families. Our fathers were on their way.

As banged up as we were, the people from the hotel drove us back to the resort untreated, put us in a room, and gave us ice for my legs and for Leonard's face. The room must have looked like a crime scene as we lay there in shock and pain, our wounds unattended, waiting for our fathers to arrive.

It was a catastrophe. In our youthful innocence and given our sense of responsibility, we thought of it as the catastrophe of wrecking the car, ruining our honeymoon, and making a mess of our lives. Would I be able to teach? Would Leonard be able to finish his studies? How could this happen?

When we finally got back to Pittsburgh, our families treated it as the catastrophe it truly was—with tears and prayers and songs expressing their gratitude to God. We had been spared. They assured us that He would watch over us, protect us, and help us heal.

That sort of faith I knew by rote. I had grown up in

the church where we prayed and sang and prayed some more for others who were in distress or need. Even so, it felt like someone dumped a bucket of ice-cold water on my head when the doctors who were treating me declared, "I'm very sorry, Mrs. Massie. It's likely you'll not be able to walk again, at least not without a great deal of difficulty and pain."

What happened in the weeks, months, and years ahead was part miracle, part determination of the sort I had learned from my grandmother. As an old West African proverb teaches, "When the music changes, so does the dance." The optimism of both our families, expressed through their faith, put our catastrophe in context. "You could have died, but God has a destiny for you, something special, so He saved you."

When people ask me how I got through any or all of my challenges, that message has played an important role. My life was spared because I had work to do. My life already had meaning—teaching was a calling I felt early. Now the stakes were higher, motivating me to live in a way that would measure up to God's expectations and to the conviction of my family that He'd saved me for a reason.

First, though, I would have to fight my way back to good health. I was determined to prove the doctors wrong.

Two:

Who Am I?

*L*ike many Americans with African ancestors, as I've gotten older I've become more interested in my family's origins. I've had the opportunity to travel quite a bit of the world and in more than one country I've had strangers tell me, "You must be from... ." It's almost always one of the West African countries— Ghana, Liberia, Ivory Coast, Mali, Nigeria—from whose shores so many slaves were shipped to the New World hundreds of years ago.

The concept that a complete stranger in a foreign country could recognize something about me and make a connection was intriguing. It's common to travel and see people you recognize as Americans, but that's not genetics, it's culture. Whether your roots are Latin American, Asian, European, or African, there are some commonalities in the way we dress and carry ourselves.

Then it happened to me—I recognized someone

else. My daughter and I were walking along a Parisian street when an older man going the other way glanced at me with smiling eyes as he passed. I felt a jolt of kinship, of familiarity. I stopped short.

"There's something about that man. I think I want to sit and talk with him a bit. Let's go back."

My daughter rolled her eyes. Talking to strangers is one of my hobbies, whether it's a waiter, a store clerk, or somebody sitting on a park bench. If the spirit moves me, I enjoy learning about the lives of others.

"Mom, you can't just go talk to a stranger in Paris. For one thing, you don't speak any French."

"Well *you* do, so come on! I'd like to just talk with him."

We caught up to the man and he smiled when I explained there was something about him that reminded me of my grandfather. "Could we sit and chat for a minute? Do you have time to spare? Can I buy you a cup of coffee?"

"Mais oui, ma fille!" Of course, daughter!

I was charmed by his response, which I assumed to be a custom wherever he was from. Many cultures use familial terms to address strangers. Chinese children traditionally call any unrelated older male "uncle," and Filipino children call middle-aged women "aunty." In African American culture, people use the terms "brother" or "sister" between unrelated adults, especially in a church setting.

When we got settled in a cafe, "uncle" said he'd had the same feeling I did when he saw me in passing. He'd thought about turning around and coming back to talk to me because, "I know you're from my country."

"Which country is that?"

"Senegal."

We had a pleasant chat and when we parted I felt so good, so connected to the distant past. It was a feeling of continuity and identity that eludes most African Americans whose ancestral trail ends at the water's edge.

My curiosity was piqued. When I got home I went through the process of having my DNA tested and matched with the region in Africa where my ancestors came from. The man in Paris had been right! My grandfather's roots were in Senegal!

How many generations of my family have come and gone since they left Africa? How many different races make up who I am—African, European, Native American? Yet I retain features that a modern day Senegalese recognizes.

The answer to the question we often ask ourselves— "Who am I?"—inevitably begins for those who live in the Americas with the question, "Where did my people come from?" This is unique to the New World. Billions of others never ask the second one because they know. The vast majority of Chinese and Indians have never set foot in another province let alone another country. Many Europeans can trace their roots back a thousand years or more, and live within a few hundred miles of where their many-times-great-grandparents lived.

The only Americans who could make such a claim are those whose ancestors were here when the rest of us showed up. Small wonder that genealogy is such a popular hobby, especially in a country that has been a magnet for people from all over the world for so long. There are few countries outside America where it would not strike the locals as odd or even an insult to be asked, "So, what are you? Italian? Irish? Hindu? Muslim?"

Americans are endlessly curious about each other's heritage, so everyone wants to be able to answer the question, "Where did your people come from?" It's an essential element in how most people define and see themselves, no matter how many generations removed they are from "the old country."

Harvard professor Henry Louis Gates Jr. turned this yearning into a popular public television series, *Finding Your Roots*. He has traced the ancestry of several dozen notable people, in some cases twenty generations back. Every one contained a surprise. Gates discovered he was half Irish.

The narrative we tell about ourselves and about our relatives—the family mythology that gives each of us a sense of being part of a continuum—plays a big role in who we decide we are, and often how we behave. During my career as an elementary school classroom teacher leading students in the study of different cultures, the kids always spotted connections to their families. "My father's German." "I'm part Italian and part Irish." "My grandparents came here from Lebanon."

Many children knew few details about their heritage but most could come up with the basics. And it clearly mattered to them that there was something unique about their families that they could talk about, something that set them apart and made them feel special.

The black children, however, would shrug and say, "I'm black, I guess. I'm African American," or maybe, "I think my mom came from Mississippi."

Some of those children, depending on what stereotype may have lodged in their minds, were ashamed to say that their heritage was African. In some families, an ancestor may have been the offspring of liaisons with slave owners who often disowned their mixed-race babies, or with Native Americans. Succeeding generations typically withheld that knowledge from children and grandchildren. Without a written record, such secrets become gaps in our links to the past.

Today, children with European roots who study their family histories can go online and look up ship manifests. The vast majority have ancestors who immigrated in the latter nineteenth and early twentieth centuries through Ellis Island, New York. The records are precise and organized and they can tell you what town their ancestors came from, the name and picture of the ship they traveled on, what class of ticket they bought, the day they arrived, how much money they had, and the first place they went after they entered the country.

These details are always fascinating, but there's more to "Who am I?" than dates, names, and locations. Who we are is shaped by family mythology—the stories we heard growing up, the sayings that are passed down through the generations, the ritual rites of passage, the beliefs and prejudices we observe and pick up from our elders without even knowing it.

There is a strong argument to be made that a positive or inspiring family mythology can motivate children to want to live up to the standards they perceive as having been set by their ancestors. Alternatively, a child who grows up with family mythology that revolves around dysfunction—violence, prison, early deaths, broken homes—can come to believe that they are doomed, a prophecy that is too easy to self-fulfill.

It was my good fortune to grow up in a family that cared about its history, took pride in it, and made sure my siblings and I knew it. My maternal family were sharecroppers in South Carolina who migrated to Pittsburgh to get away from the dangers of life for black folks living in the Deep South.

One of the stories I remember hearing as a youngster

was about the time my grandmother was hoeing in a field when one of the white men who lived nearby accosted her and tried to have his way with her. The story goes that my grandmother brandished her hoe, ready to strike, and warned, "If you touch me, you will be a dead man on this field. You better get out of here like you have some sense and never come back." She'd apparently said it with enough conviction that her would-be attacker fled. In any case, the incident left a powerful impression on my mother and her siblings, and it was passed on to me.

Years later, when the television miniseries *Roots* was broadcast in 1977, telling the story of one family from its roots in Gambia through the Civil War, my grandmother refused to watch. "I lived it! It's too painful."

My grandparents finally left South Carolina in 1941, moving to Pittsburgh. They were following in the footsteps of a great-uncle and other relatives at the beginning of what some scholars have called the second Great Migration of African Americans, leaving the South to move to the northern cities where jobs were plentiful.

Although the schools and neighborhoods around Pittsburgh were just as segregated and discrimination was just as common, "At least they weren't going to take us out in the woods and hang us from a tree," as my mother put it. "It wasn't the Deep South, but we did call it the Up South."

A few years after they moved in, the houses in the white section were being repainted but not the houses where the black families lived. My grandmother badgered management to come paint her house. After her requests had been ignored one too many times, she went down to the rental office one day in the late 1940s and handcuffed herself to a radiator pipe, promising she wouldn't leave until she got what everybody else got. And she did. Stories like that shaped my self-image and gave me courage many times when it was needed.

My generation came of age in the 1960s, a period of rapid change. My experiences ranged from the sort of racism I encountered in second grade—when a teacher scolded a white girl for using her comb on my hair—to being abandoned on a gurney in the hallway of a hospital emergency room on my honeymoon, with shattered knees and a husband who had apparently returned from the dead.

In between, I drew on my family mythology as modeled by my grandmother's sense of justice and her intense faith. That got me through some moments that, in retrospect, were more Deep South than Up South.

Three:

Living Up South

*D*uring my senior year of high school I experienced two very public indignities that even my grandmother couldn't fix.

Both incidents occurred just as the civil rights movement was in full-throated cry. President Lyndon Johnson had just signed the Civil Rights Act of 1964, a historic moment that, in context, was almost as profound and controversial as the Emancipation Proclamation a century earlier.

You would have thought that the Pittsburgh area, where white folks and black folks had been working side by side in the steel mills and machine shops since World War II, might have been ahead of the social curve. That perception of safety and opportunity was what had lured our family out of the Jim Crow South. It was a big improvement, but no Promised Land. Our elders joked that they had aimed to move Up North but only got as far as Up South.

By the time I graduated in 1968, there had been just one black teacher on the staff of West Mifflin North High School and one black teacher in one of the elementary schools—my mother's sister, my Aunt Gwen. Gwen was the first groundbreaker in our family. She was the first to earn a college degree at a time when high school guidance counselors discouraged black children from harboring such aspirations.

That had been Gwen's experience. Her goal from childhood was to become a teacher. Her mother, my grandmother, had arranged for Gwen to attend an elementary school where she ended up being the only black student.

One day in fifth grade she mentioned her dream. The news left her teacher momentarily speechless. Then she recovered and said brightly, "Well, that's wonderful, Gwen; and you know that Down South they need a lot of good teachers, and you would be a wonderful teacher there."

Gwen thought, *My mother and father brought our family here to get away from Down South. Why would I want to go back there?* Her teacher's reaction was so deflating that from then on she kept her plans to herself. She even avoided joining a Future Teachers of America group because she figured it was only for the white students.

Gwen was more of an older sister to me than an aunt. She is only nine years my senior, so her success was a tangible and hopeful sign of progress for the younger relatives and a source of pride in our community. On the other hand, there were daily reminders that we still lived in a dual society.

For example, the school bus that picked up the kids from the Whitaker Projects would come and get all the white kids first, drop them off at school, and then return for us black kids. If it was cold, snowy, or raining, we were expected to wait out in the weather until the bus returned. We complained but the practice continued as long as I was a student.

The district no doubt wanted to avoid confrontations at a time when every city in the country with a sizable African American community was on edge, especially in hot weather. The first of what would turn out to be a wave of massive, deadly riots had taken place in Los Angeles the summer before my sophomore year. The LA riot had begun with a routine traffic stop that exploded into an uprising against the nearly all-white police department, which had a reputation for being callous, corrupt, and brutal. "Race riot" entered the daily lexicon and the next summer, 1966, saw similar outbreaks of violence, arson, and looting in more than three dozen cities across the country.

A record-breaking heat wave had baked western Pennsylvania that summer, but Pittsburgh had been spared. An article later that year in the *Pittsburgh Courier*, the black-owned newspaper, attributed the peace to a better-than-average economy and complacency. It was true that black people in the Pittsburgh area were a little less poor than those in some other cities. But downtown department stores still refused to hire "Negroes," certain labor unions refused them membership, and factory owners often set limits on how many African Americans they would employ.

Our home economics teacher let the white kids cook and assigned us black kids to cut, chop, and clean up. Fortunately, we had a thoughtful principal, Mr. Benyak, who heard me out when I took him our complaint and encouraged me to bring these injustices to his attention when they happened. One day he made a surprise visit to home-ec, saw what was going on, and after that we weren't treated as kitchen help.

A huge personal indignity was the outcome of an essay I had written that was submitted by one of my teachers for a scholarship contest sponsored by the Daughters of the American Revolution (DAR). The DAR, founded in 1890, describes itself today as "a volunteer women's service organization dedicated to promoting patriotism, preserving American history, and securing America's future through better education for children."

In the 1960s, however, membership was limited to those who could trace their lineage to a person who contributed to the independence of the United States—so long as they were white. Black people were completely excluded until 1977 when Karen Batchelor, a young black woman from Detroit, documented her family history to a patriot who served in the colonial militia in Pennsylvania.

All I knew was that the DAR was a prestigious organization and it was a singular honor to have had my essay chosen out of thousands that were submitted from around the country. Even better, three representatives of the DAR were going to come to our school to personally give it to me during a school-wide assembly in the auditorium.

The big day arrived, the three ladies came on stage, and when I heard my name I jumped out of my seat and walked proudly down the aisle, around to the side steps, up on the stage, and took my place next to my English teacher. I was nearly breathless with excitement, grinning ear to ear.

It didn't register with me right away that the three women were no longer smiling. In fact, their faces had a frozen look, with raised eyebrows and pinched mouths.

They went into a huddle, backs to the audience. My English teacher leaned in to investigate. A dark look crossed his face. Arms waved and fingers wagged. My stomach churned.

Finally, another teacher gently took me by the arm. "Come on, Elfreda. Let's go backstage so we can talk."

Behind the curtain, with the auditorium of restless teenagers becoming noisier by the second, he explained that it was against the DAR policy to give a scholarship to a black student. They had clearly been thrown off by my last name, Winstead, which is English and was given to my ancestors when they were slaves.

The audience was starting to figure out what was going on and a few voices were raised: "That's not fair! It's not right!" The murmurs gave way to shouting. Then the students started walking out in protest. My bright shining moment had been snatched away.

There were many moments like that for all of us, some more subtle than others. It was just the way things were. Out of nearly 200 students in my graduating class, fewer than a dozen were black.

The white kids may have taken my side in the DAR incident, but when it came to traditions like homecoming, it was still Up South. That fall, 1966, I was one of three finalists for homecoming queen, and the first black girl ever. One of my teachers told me that I had gotten the most votes. That meant I was going to be the first-ever African American to be West Mifflin North High School's homecoming queen!

But when the official announcement was made, the name was not mine but one of the other two girls, both of whom were white. I was crushed. The teacher who had tipped me off called my mother and confirmed what we already knew. "It's not right. She got the most votes.

She was elected homecoming queen. But some of the teachers felt it wasn't the time to have a Negro girl be homecoming queen."

The homecoming king was a white boy and the prospect of a mixed-race homecoming couple must have been so provocative as to be unthinkable. My grandmother paid one of her visits to the school, but the decision stood. Instead I got the consolation prize—they made me the queen's number two. I'd still get to dress up and be part of the ceremonies.

I had been raised to do your best and accept what life throws at you without holding grudges or harboring ill feelings. It's the way things are, I told myself, but it'll change one day. It's not always going to be like this, and the fact that I've made it this far is something to be proud of.

In fact, number two was pretty good. I got to ride in a convertible around the football stadium during the ceremonies before the big game. I needed a special dress for such a public occasion, a luxury my family couldn't afford. But I had a beloved godmother, Miss Katie Barnes, who took me shopping whenever I needed a new dress for a prom or a dance. She would later buy me my wedding dress.

Miss Barnes lived next door to the church and was always there on Sundays, when she played the piano, and for special occasions during the week. She was an important and somewhat exotic presence in my life. She was so fair-skinned it was hard to tell that she was black. Her family was well-off and, unlike anyone else we knew, she and her husband lived in a real house. They had no children of their own. She was also a generous and doting presence. When my sister and I wanted to get our hair pressed for a special occasion, we'd go to her house and she'd do it for us for free. In return, we cleaned and ran her errands.

For the homecoming festivities, Miss Barnes helped me pick out a dress that I immediately fell in love with—dark green faux suede at the top and light green silky material at the bottom. I'd never owned such a beautiful dress and the prospect of wearing it in front of the whole school at the big game was thrilling.

On game day, the car I was riding in followed the queen's car as we rolled past our home team bleachers. The band was playing, the people in the bleachers were holding pennants and clapping, and I was waving to my friends with a white-gloved hand when someone punched me in the shoulder, or so it felt. I also felt something wet on my cheek. I looked down to find my beautiful skirt splattered with the slimy yolk and albumen of an egg. A piece of shell fell off my shoulder into my lap. Then it began to hail eggs and tomatoes.

People often ask me what I felt at that moment. The cruelty of it is overwhelming, especially to white folks. Black folks are more likely to shrug and say, "Yeah. That's the way it was, all right." Just about every African American alive at that time can tell a similar, if less dramatic, anecdote.

The suddenness and violence of the attack—people were trying to hurt me and they had destroyed my dress—was surreal. Things like that didn't happen to actual people, only on television or in the movies. This can't be happening. My beautiful dress! Ruined, in front of the whole school!

My face blazed and then I got goose bumps when it hit me that some crazy person might come down out of the stands and actually attack me. All those emotions boiled over at once and I just sat there paralyzed, like a rabbit trying to make itself invisible. It was a moment of such utter humiliation that people often ask me why I don't seem bitter about it. Answering that question has been one of the catalysts for writing this book.

You might say the bitterness was loved out of me by my family and faith. When bad things happened, we'd have a family caucus—us kids and my parents and grandparents. We'd all talk about what happened, why it happened, what we should do, and, of course, we'd pray about it.

The message was clear—we were people who refused to let meanness and injustice tear us down. Our spiritual roots played a central role in how we were taught to treat other people. We never talked about turning the other cheek, but we did talk about the Golden Rule and always tried to carry ourselves with dignity, no matter how great the indignity.

This concept of family narrative and how it defines us was explored in the mid-1990s by Marshall Duke, a psychologist at Emory University who investigated the role played by myth and ritual. "There was a lot of research at the time into the dissipation of the family," he told the *New York Times* in 2013. "We were more interested in what families could do to counteract those forces."

Dr. Duke's wife, Sara, a psychologist who works with children with learning disabilities, noticed that children who know a lot about their families tended to do better when they faced challenges. Dr. Duke and a colleague developed a measure called the "Do You Know?" scale that asked children to answer questions such as: Do you know where your grandparents grew up? Do you know where your mom and dad went to high school? Do you know where your parents met? Do you know an illness or something really terrible that happened in your family? Do you know the story of your birth?

They compared the results with psychological tests and concluded that the more children knew about their family's history, the stronger their sense of control over their lives, the greater their self-esteem, and the more successfully they believed their families functioned.

One of the dominant ideas in the field of family psychology is that every family has a unifying narrative that takes one of three basic shapes.

The ascending narrative is the one about the poor immigrant (or migrant, in the case of my family) who arrives with nothing, opens a store, and the succeeding generations stand on the shoulders of those who came before.

The descending narrative is the one in which a family was wealthy and lost it all.

"The most healthful narrative," Dr. Duke told the *Times*, "is the oscillating family narrative that describes the daily ups and downs, the disasters, and the lost jobs, the relatives who went to jail, and so on." It ends, he said, with the message, 'But we always stuck together as a family.'"

Ours was both an ascending and healthful narrative. Like my Aunt Gwen, there was never any question that my siblings and cousins and I were expected to go to college. I did my best to live up to that expectation. My senior year my grades put me in the top ten percent of my class and my SAT scores were also well above average. I felt confident enough that I wanted to apply to several Ivy League colleges knowing I might be their first or second black student.

Eager to make my mark on the world, I believed I could take on any challenge. I didn't have to wait long to find out. When I sat down with my guidance counselor to discuss the schools I wanted to apply to, she shook her head woefully.

"You really should consider going to a junior college." She assured me that trying to get into any of those prestigious schools would be an exercise in futility. I was just setting myself up for disappointment.

I listened and kept my thoughts to myself, then brought this news home where it was met with appropriate indignation and recognition. Aunt Gwen recalled how outraged the family was the day she came home from school and at dinner asked, "Why do I have to go Down South to be a teacher?"

Her uncle, who was eating with them, exploded with a few choice words. My grandparents told her, "That's ridiculous. You can be whatever you want." They had all been upset, and the incident left a lasting impression on Gwen.

My grandmother's singular, passionate, and deeply personal mission was to see her children and grandchildren go to college and not have to clean other people's toilets for a living. As a child, growing up in South Carolina, she had loved being a student but the local primary school for black children only went up to the eighth grade. The nearest black secondary school was too far away to consider commuting. The family had no relatives there who could offer her a place to stay and there was no money for books.

My grandmother avoided talking about the bad old days in front of us kids. If one of us walked into the room when she was talking about some incident that happened in the past, she'd clam up. Nevertheless, we all grew up knowing the one story that was most important to us: the day she graduated from eighth grade she stood in front of the school, sobbing.

When she became a mother, she was determined that her children have what she could not. Moving to Pennsylvania had been the first step. My grandparents working two or three jobs for years helped pay for Gwen's college. As she grew up, Gwen did her share of cleaning as well. We all did. When it was time for Gwen to decide on colleges to attend, it came down to either Duquesne University or the University of Pittsburgh.

My grandmother asked her which one she preferred.

"Duquesne is all right," Gwen said. "I like Pitt, but Duquesne is less expensive."

"If you want to go to Pitt, you go to Pitt. We'll figure out how to pay for it." And they did.

With support at home, I ignored my guidance counselor and submitted applications to several schools, including Sarah Lawrence and Radcliffe. Waiting for the replies was nerve-wracking and exciting, until the first one arrived—a rejection. Then one after the other came back, all rejections. Not one of the Ivy League schools would have me.

My grandmother said what everyone was thinking. "Something's not right about this. We need to talk to those colleges and find out what's going on."

You never get used to racial discrimination and insensitivity, but even for us, who had experienced enough, what we learned was a shocker. The admissions directors told us they had received a letter from my guidance counselor saying I was only in the fiftieth percentile of my class. The counselor had lied for no other possible purpose but sabotage.

My grandmother put on her good hat and marched the two miles up the hill to the high school to read my guidance counselor the riot act, cite some scripture, and set the record straight. When the dust had settled, Sarah Lawrence did accept me.

It was a victory, but the struggle to get there got me thinking. I weighed the prestige and opportunity against the prospect of going into a new environment, far from home, without my family at my side, being one of a few black students, possibly the only one. Nobody would know about me nor my grandmother. My behavior and my grades would be closely observed.

Who could say how many more of these battles would have to be fought? In the end, I decided I wanted my college years to be free of that sort of stress. I wanted a break from being a pioneer.

My safety schools, the University of Pittsburgh and Pennsylvania State University, had accepted me as well. Penn State was a distance from home, in the middle of the rural center of the state. Pitt was twenty minutes from the Whitaker Projects. I knew I would be one of many black students, and that I could live on campus and start to have some independence but go home any time. Pitt was where my Aunt Gwen had earned her undergraduate degree and the admissions staff was excited to have me follow in her footsteps. It turned out to be a good match.

These and other experiences cemented the importance of my family's narrative in my life. It has sustained me through some difficult times. I have been able to pass it on to my daughters who, a generation later, had to deal with some of the same kinds of racial insensitivity and all the rest of life's challenges. Things are getting better, but there's plenty of work to be done.

Family mythology is something over which we as parents and grandparents have more control than we realize. A child raised in a family whose narrative thread includes violence, substance abuse, abandonment, incarceration, and so on is more likely to think of him- or herself as doomed. A child raised in a home where the response to injustice or disappointment is rage is more likely to grow up angry.

So when people ask me why I'm not bitter about some of the challenges I've had to face, I tell them my grandparents created out of nothing more than faith and good intentions an ascending family narrative that gave me the courage and the confidence to keep going. My grandmother in particular shaped that narrative by the stories she told and the stories she didn't—the ones she'd stop telling in mid-sentence if one of us kids happened to come into the room.

Some experts suggest families write a mission statement to identify core values. The various branches of the military draw on their family narratives by teaching recruits about the history of the service, visiting cemeteries, exploring vintage weapons, and so on.

Bruce Feiler, author of *The Secrets of Happy Families*, says happy families talk through problems by telling positive stories about themselves. "The bottom line: if you want a happier family, create, refine, and retell the story of your family's positive moments and your ability to bounce back from the difficult ones. That act alone may increase the odds that your family will thrive for many generations to come."

Amen.

Four:

The Stream Never Forgets

My college career began in September 1968, a year of such upheaval, fear, and violence that it required an extra measure of faith and youthful optimism to keep from feeling the world was just spinning out of control. I had plenty of both.

Each week nearly 300 American soldiers were dying in Vietnam and another 1,700 were wounded. More than 15,000 young men would die that year, making it the bloodiest of the war. Everyone in the Pittsburgh area seemed to know someone who had died or was wounded, in harm's way, or facing the draft.

That year the civil rights movement lost its three most powerful leaders. Organized anti-war protests had forced President Lyndon Johnson, instrumental in passage of the 1964, 1965, and 1968 Civil Rights Acts, to abandon his re-election bid and thus become a lame duck.

In April, Dr. Martin Luther King Jr., who had

given such hope and a voice to so many, was murdered by an assassin. His death broke many of our hearts and triggered riots in every major city. Frustrated African Americans took their grief and rage out on their own neighborhoods, breaking windows and setting fires with Molotov cocktails to businesses owned by blacks as well as whites.

All across the country, National Guard units were called up and deployed to the inner cities to restore order. In Pittsburgh alone, more than 6,000 soldiers in full military gear occupied streets where some 500 buildings burned, often because firefighters refused to go into certain neighborhoods for fear of being shot.

The city streets resembled a war zone with patrols of olive green transport trucks and jeeps bristling with rifles mixed in with ordinary traffic and people going about their lives. What had been a thriving business section in the Hill District, where most of the city's black families lived and shopped, was destroyed. Nearly fifty years later, it still hadn't recovered.

Two months after Dr. King's death, an assassin murdered another civil rights advocate: presidential candidate Robert F. Kennedy, the former US Attorney General whose brother, President John F. Kennedy, had himself been murdered just five years earlier. In August, at the Democratic National Convention in Chicago, some 10,000 student protesters chanting "The whole world is watching!" were tear-gassed and beaten by the police on live television.

Against this backdrop, I arrived at Pitt that summer, just before starting my freshman year. I was accepted to work in a program called Upward Bound that provided academic support to the growing number of first-year minority students. After a failed attempt at a job as a typist, I was assigned instead to be a reading and math tutor working with students who were often older than me. It was a perfect fit.

Seeing the "aha" moments when my tutees learned new concepts was exhilarating. I was going to be an education major and the experience confirmed that I had made the right career choice. My Aunt Sybil worked at Carlow College, where the program was housed, so the added benefit was that she took me to lunch every day and we had "grown-up" conversations about life and love.

Inspired in part by my Aunt Gwen, teaching had been my calling for as long as I could remember. I loved school, idolized most of my teachers, and from an early age had worked as a babysitter in the neighborhood, using my time with young children showing them how to read and write.

When I reached junior high, my mother had become an administrator for the federal Head Start preschool program office in Pittsburgh. Head Start employed student interns and my mother recruited them from our neighborhood, myself included. She provided many teens in our neighborhood the opportunity to make a little money and serve our community. I began to realize that my mother had many of the traits I admired in my grandmother.

That fall of 1968 the black students at Pitt got together and formed the Black Action Society—still in existence today—which, among other activities, staged class boycotts and demonstrations to draw attention to our issues. The organization's preamble includes a lovely proverb, believed to have originated in Africa, that had special meaning for me: "No matter how far a stream flows, it never forgets its source." And as a corresponding proverb puts it, "A river that forgets its source will soon dry up."

The source of my river at that point in my life could be said to have been my great-grandfather, who I never met but knew from family lore had been an educated preacher in South Carolina and a leader in the community. In my daily life, the source was my grandmother, the young girl who had been deprived of a complete education and channeled her frustration into a life force that flowed through her children, her grandchildren, and later, when I became a mother, through me to her great-grandchildren.

That family narrative—the source of my river—was so important to me that when the Black Action Society announced a class boycott on a day when I had to take an important test, I found myself with a dilemma. I wanted to show my solidarity but I would have to take the exam, a decision that left me ostracized by a few classmates.

"You don't understand my family thing," I pleaded. "My mother and my grandmother aren't going to excuse a C for any reason, no matter how righteous." My solution was to race through the exam as fast as I could and then dash off to the student union where the black students were holding their rally.

In January of 1969, I participated in a historic sit-in at the university, led by the Black Action Society. About fifty black students took over the computer center. When it was over, the university agreed to admit more African American students and hire more African American professors. Our protest sparked similar actions at the surrounding colleges and universities, and similar changes in admission and hiring practices.

From just about the time I was old enough to handle a dust rag and began helping my grandmother clean her customer's homes, I had worked. When I was a little older, I began babysitting, and later had all sorts of jobs, continuing to work all through college to supplement my student loans and partial scholarship. I read textbooks to a blind student, babysat an instructor's child, and proof-read journals for a law firm.

When the new sports arena—Three Rivers Stadium— opened in July 1970, I applied and was hired as one of two dozen "Stadium Girl" usherettes earning $2 an hour. We had to learn about the history of the Pittsburgh Pirates and be able to explain about the redevelopment project that helped fund the new facility.

We wore mini-skirted black-and-gold uniforms with white faux-leather go-go boots. We were sometimes assigned to serve the famous fans and their families who watched the Pittsburgh Steelers football games and Pirates baseball games from box seats. The generous tips made that one of my better-paying jobs, and certainly the most exciting.

I worked the box used by legendary Pirates right-fielder Roberto Clemente, a Puerto Rican who, in the days when players stayed put, spent his entire eighteen-year career in Pittsburgh. I got to know his family and entertained the kids who were too young to be interested in the games. Clemente's career was famously cut short when he died in a plane crash.

I also worked the box of first baseman Willie Stargell, a star black player who would stay in Pittsburgh for twenty years before retiring. When celebrities came to town, like black comedienne Jackie "Moms" Mabley and singer Aretha Franklin, they'd often show up in one of the boxes and we got to see them up close, exchange a few words, and go home with some serious bragging rights.

"Moms" Mabley (born Loretta Mary Aiken) was a

particular favorite at the time, a black entertainer who'd lost both her parents when she was young, was raped at the age of fourteen, ran away to join the vaudeville circuit, and went on to become one of the top-paid entertainers of her time—black or white. In the 1930s she was the first woman entertainer to come out of the closet as a lesbian and perform stand-up routines about it.

By the time I encountered Mabley, she was in her seventies and still working, dressed in her signature frumpy flowered dress and knit cap, telling edgy ethnocentric jokes that were hilarious. Once dubbed "The Funniest Woman In The World," she'd played Carnegie Hall and was a regular on top television variety shows. Although working "blue" (telling off-color jokes) much of her career, by the late 1960s she began to close her performances with a variation on a Frank Sinatra hit, "My Way," changing the repeated lyric to, "I tried to do it His way."

She'd had a hit recording in 1969 of "Abraham, Martin, and John," a 1968 folk-rock tune first recorded by Dion about the assassinations of Lincoln, Kennedy, Dr. King, and Bobby Kennedy. The repeated lyric became famous: "It seems the good die young." With the murders of Bobby and Dr. King still painfully fresh, it was impossible to listen to her emotional rendition without getting weepy.

At a time in history that was brimming with tragedy, work and school were positive distractions. I kept myself so busy that I had little time to contemplate the woes of the world. I earned enough working my part-time jobs that I was able to put myself through college on the fast track. I took as many as twenty-one credits some semesters and also took courses in the summer so I wouldn't have to move home and lose my momentum. As a result,

I finished in three years instead of four, graduating in 1971 at the age of twenty.

To fulfill my student-teaching requirement during my last year at Pitt, I was assigned to an all-black elementary school in the Hill District, working with a kindergarten teacher who was about thirty years old. When I walked into the classroom the first day, I was shocked to find the class totally out of order with five- and six-year-olds running around the room, shouting and screaming their heads off. One kid was chasing the teacher with a yardstick.

After two days of watching how helpless she seemed, I felt I had to do something. When two kids started fighting, I asked her, "Do you want me to break that up?"

"Oh, no! You can't intervene in a fight."

Maybe YOU can't, I thought, but I can and will.

Since all the children were black and the teacher was white and had no cultural experience to draw on, and with racial sensitivity so high at the time, she must have been intimidated about disciplining them. I wasn't intimidated and I did have the cultural tools, so I was thrilled when she took a leave of absence and the principal asked me to take over the class.

The first day on my own I laid down some serious rules, like my grandmother had for me, instilling a bit of the fear of God in them in the process. I let them know that if they breathed or looked at me wrong we were going to have big, big trouble. That and the fact that I looked and sounded like their elders at home produced an immediate change in behavior. They began to show respect, listen, and follow the rules.

During my student teaching assignment, Leonard and I had become a couple. He was studying math and computer sciences at the University of Maryland and when he came home to visit I took him with me to school. The kids loved him. He has a warm, embracing personality and he was a rarity, a black male teacher in an elementary school. The experience gave him the bug. He went back to the University of Maryland and switched his major from mathematics to elementary education.

In my final months at Pitt I attended a job fair after which I had three offers—one to teach in an elementary school in Baltimore County, Maryland, and one in Atlanta, Georgia, and one to become an airline stewardess. The allure of travel was tantalizing. I yearned to see the world. But then love walked in.

Five:

Throwing The First Stone

*L*eonard swears he fell in love the first time I threw
pebbles at him. From that rocky start our lives
slowly converged during seven or eight years from
adolescence to young adulthood, ending a bit like a
fairy tale—the humble, patient prince finally wins the
hand of the elusive princess.

We first met when his family moved into the end
unit of the row of homes next to the row we lived in,
also in an end unit. Our houses were separated by a
wide swatch of yard that served as playground and
park. That made the end units noisier but it also meant
having open space on three sides, only one neighbor,
and cross ventilation.

Leonard was the only boy of the five Massie
children. Mr. Massie had a steady union job in one of
the mills. As the family grew, he took on odd jobs to
keep all those hungry chicks fed.

Leonard's mother kept house, so he grew up

surrounded by females. Between what he learned from the women in his life and the strict rules about proper behavior that his father laid down, Leonard was raised to be a gentleman. The other kids thought he was nerdy, and that made him somewhat shy.

In spite of our similar cultural backgrounds and being just a month apart in age, we were about as different as ice and steam. He was solid and reliable, a rock. I was spirited and social, a songbird.

We were only twelve years old when Leonard first declared to my bemused grandmother that one day he was going to marry me. I laughed it off. He was just one of the neighborhood boys, a loner, not in my posse of friends. He had one best friend but beyond that he mostly kept to himself or worked—he was never without a least one job and helped his father with his handyman work.

He and I first noticed each other soon after the Massies moved in. More precisely, I noticed him noticing me. Being rather sure of myself and fiercely independent, I had an irresistible urge to act out my feelings. One afternoon when he was out in front of his house with his bike, stealing glances at me as he folded the newspapers and stuffed them into his bag, I collected a bunch of stones and sat down on our front steps, waiting.

When Leonard finally set out on his route, as he passed in front of our house he turned and grinned at me just as I threw a pebble at him, and then another and another, just for the pleasure of annoying him and letting him know his place. Those pebbles became the seeds of a lifelong partnership.

His father, Leonard Percy Massie, was originally from Lynchburg, Virginia. After serving in the Army during World War II, he settled in Pittsburgh, which was just coming off a wartime industrial boom. He married Leonard's mother when she was just seventeen. Mr. Massie was himself a rock, a reliable protector and provider, and a stoic family patriarch. He never said much, but when he did speak Leonard and his four sisters knew it was time to listen.

Many of the working-age men in our neighborhood had jobs like Leonard's father, down the hill from the river bluff where the Whitaker projects had been built. Three hundred feet down in the valley, the wide, slow Monongahela River—"river with crumbling banks," the Native Americans called it—flows in sweeping bends for fifteen miles until it reaches Pittsburgh. Its confluence there with the Allegheny River is the starting point of the Ohio River, the 1,300-mile artery that connects with the Mississippi at Cairo, Illinois.

Hugging the banks of "the Mon," as we called it, on a narrow plain between the foot of the bluffs and the water's edge, were miles of steam- and soot-belching steel mills, foundries, and fabricating plants interspersed with sprawling railyards and docks sprouting huge cranes. Coal came downstream from West Virginia, iron ore came upstream from Lake Superior by way of Cleveland. The finished rolls of steel sheet and other products went back downstream to market.

Both banks of the river had been industrialized except for one section near us where the lights of Kennywood, a popular amusement park, lit the summer night sky. When the wind was right, you could hear the periodic screams of the coaster riders as they began the big drops.

U.S. Steel's Homestead Works, site of one of the earliest and most important strikes in the history of the labor movement, was just a mile and a half from where we lived. The rail yards were only 500 yards or so down the steep, wooded hillsides. The hard sounds of heavy industry echoed up and down the valley day and night—the banging, screeching, and whistling of trains and the periodic roar of furnaces. Steel provided the underscore of our lives, lulling us to sleep at night and waking us in the morning.

Steel also fed the Massie family, but as it grew Leonard's father took on odd jobs. When Leonard was old enough, he took him along as a helper. Like my parents, Leonard's mother and father had high expectations for him.

Now and then a customer would shortchange his father or take advantage of him in some other way. When Leonard groused—"Hey, Dad, this just ain't fair!"—Mr. Massie told him, "In this world you're always going to be swimming among sharks. Make sure you don't let them see you bleed."

That was the message most black kids heard growing up, in one form or another, and still do. In those days just about every black parent told their kids some variation on that theme. "If you're running a hundred-yard race against a white guy, just remember that he has a fifty-yard head start. You have to do twice as well just to keep up."

Back when we were still in junior high, my parents moved us up the slope, to a house at the top. It was a good spot, above the smoky valley where the air was freshest. But the house was old, threadbare, and dark, like the scary house in the original thriller *Psycho*, which had just come out and been a huge sensation. In the Jects, this had become the neighborhood's "old haunted house up the hill."

My father, Wheeler Winstead Sr., saw an opportunity. The house just needed a happy family to move in and someone good with a hammer and saw. That was us. When he wasn't at his job in the steel mill, my father built houses for other people, from foundations to chimneys. So he went to work tearing down the wallpaper, patching and painting, extending rooms, building a porch, adding a bathroom.

In Leonard's view, however, I became one of the "rich" kids, an uptown girl, while he remained a downtown boy. We attended different junior highs and saw less of each other for a couple of years. When we reached high school, we saw each other every day. We were two of just a couple dozen black students out of about 1,500.

Leonard developed into a gifted athlete and, in spite of his shyness, was elected captain of the varsity basketball, baseball, and football teams. When it came time to hand out the MVP trophies, they always went to the white boys. Being in such a small minority and having shared experiences of being cheated out of what we earned—that award from the Daughters of the American Revolution, for example—Leonard and I had a lot in common and became great friends.

Like I did, he would come home from his bitter experiences with an ache in his heart. His father assured him, "You're going to get your recognition when it counts. I'm sure you're going to get into college on a scholarship and then you're going to be all right and none of this will matter anymore."

Mr. Massie was right. Both Penn State and the University of Maryland were eager to recruit Leonard. Penn State was in the middle of nowhere, a long, lonely drive from Pittsburgh to an isolated college town that was overwhelmingly white. He was offered a generous scholarship at the University of Maryland, just outside Washington, DC, and that was where he decided to earn his undergraduate degree.

It took me quite a while to take Leonard's romantic

attention seriously. He was Mr. Straight and Narrow while I used to sneak out of the house at night with my girlfriends to go to parties. Leonard made himself hard to dismiss. He treated me with respect as though I were a beautiful young lady (which was not how I saw myself) and smart (which I knew).

His father had trained him well. "If you go out with a woman, you've got to open doors for her. If you go out in her car, you've got to fill the gas tank before you take her home."

Singing was one of my principal passions. My grandmother disapproved of anything but church music. So I used to sneak out to go to the Rankin Club, an Elks Lodge for blacks on the other side of the Mon, where I got a chance to sneak out and sing with my brother, Wheeler, and a group of other musicians.

One of my favorites was Satin Doll, a jazz standard composed by Duke Ellington with racy lyrics by Johnny Mercer: "Cigarette holder which wigs me, Over her shoulder, she digs me."

One night, in the middle of Satin Doll, I spotted in the audience a familiar face that made my stomach flop. I was in a club, where I wasn't supposed to be, underage, with Miss Graham, one of my mother's friends, glaring at me. I managed to stumble my way through the rest of the song and fled, knowing that the news would reach my mother before I did. There were consequences, but I was willful and it happened more than once.

"You can't go out of the house for three weeks," my mother would say. Or, "The next two parties that you want to go to, you have to stay home." She had no idea when these parties were supposed to be, so I just pretended there was one and did my best to put on a sullen face.

Leonard and I became best friends in high school

after I got into a fight with a boy I was seeing. I punched him petty hard (I can't remember why) and the rumor mill ginned the story up until it had me pushing him off a cliff. The word got out: don't mess with Elfreda.

That suited Leonard just fine. He'd been dating a girl he wasn't that interested in so he and I became closer, especially in our senior year. He was a big deal on the football team—the Vikings—and I was the only black girl on the marching drill team—the Vikettes. He was in the locker room during halftime when the white kids ruined my homecoming outfit by throwing eggs at me. He was beside himself when he found out—angry but helpless. It was just the way things were and nothing could be done about it.

After graduation he went off to school in Maryland and I began my undergraduate degree at Pitt. By taking summer courses, I shortened my college career by a year, and his was going to take almost five years. So he was in his junior year when I was about to graduate and looking into my options.

At a job fair I attended I talked to some representatives from airline companies looking to hire cabin attendants. I'd loved being a Stadium Girl at Three Rivers, meeting and taking care of people. Working for an airline seemed like that kind of a fun job with the huge added benefit of getting to see some of the world and meeting new people. In addition to applying for teaching positions, I submitted some airline applications. Being an airline stewardess was not a lifelong career in those days. When I got tired of it, I figured I could still go into my first love, teaching, and settle down.

When I got a call from American Airlines offering me a spot I was ecstatic. I also was offered teaching positions in Baltimore County, Maryland, and in Atlanta,

Georgia, but I had travel on my mind. I called Leonard at college to tell him the good news. His response was subdued and the next weekend he drove up, took me out, and proposed.

It must have been hell for him because it took me a week or so to think about it. He was my best friend and in some ways I had thought of him like a brother. In the end I decided that marrying your best friend made sense. I hated having to do it but I turned down the American Airlines job. Since Leonard was going to be at school in Maryland for another year or so, I accepted the Baltimore County job and we were married during spring break in 1972.

We were both twenty-one years old when the car we were riding in on our way home from our honeymoon hit a tree on a dark, icy mountain road, launching Leonard through the windshield into a ditch and me out the passenger door into a pasture. After we had been ignored in the emergency room at the hospital, the hotel where we stayed sent someone over to pick us up and take us back to await our fathers, who were driving up together from home.

It's funny now, but our fathers were not amused when it was decided to leave in the morning and the hotel gave them a room with one double bed. In between their anguish at our condition and their relief that we were alive, they squabbled over who would have to sleep on the floor because, "There's no way I'm sharing a heart-shaped bed with a man!"

The accident turned our world upside down but our families showed us how to deal with it. Leonard, whose injuries were less severe, felt terrible about what happened to me and about destroying our car.

Our parents and grandparents prayed with us every day and whenever either of us began feeling sorry for ourselves, we were reminded that either or both of us could have died. This confirmed for them that God had "something special for you, a destiny." They just kept repeating, "Everything is going to be all right, and God's going to do this, God is going to do that."

It took Leonard longer than it took me to get from "we just made a mess of our lives" to "God saved us." Leonard was a believer, but he had not yet accepted the call. "I thank God I've still got my limbs," he'd say. "I thank God I've still got my wife. We are still alive." After that, it was a matter of evolution. "Rather than a calling," he says today, "I had a nudging that became a calling as we visited churches looking for one to join."

Once we found a church in Baltimore we liked, it was second nature to use our talents—my singing and Leonard's love for the gospel. His calling became clearer. Leonard has since become a pastor and talks about discovering "the comfort level with who you are, how God is using you, and then ultimately how you are blessing others when you're used, whether it's through a prayer, a song, or pastoral work."

Our lives together began with a great test of our faith. I thank God we didn't know how many more tests lay ahead.

Part II
The Power of Love

Six:

If You Can't Walk, Crawl

I returned from our honeymoon with a shattered knee and other injuries that doctors told me would prevent me from ever walking normally again.

I was only twenty-one, too young and strong-willed to accept such a judgment without a fight. From the time I was paddled in second grade for letting a white girl comb my hair, I had developed an instinct for knowing when to pick my fights. This time, at least, it wasn't about the color of my skin. It would, however, be about my body, my belief in myself, and my faith in God.

You can't go through such an experience without wondering what sort of plan He had in mind that included crippling an athletic young woman just as she was beginning what should be the best years of her life. How did I suddenly become so unlucky?

On the other hand, as our families and friends repeatedly told us with overflowing hearts and eyes full of hope, Leonard and I must have been spared for some greater purpose, yet to be revealed. It was such a comforting thought and a reminder that when you find yourself going through Hell, as the saying goes, don't stop to take pictures. Just keep going!

In my family of humble stoics we tell each other to take a day to cry—and then get back to the business of living. Much later, when my daughters were growing up and complaining about some disappointment, I'd tell them, "Take the day to scream and cry and do what you need to do. But there's going to be daylight again and every morning brings new mercies and beginnings. What's happened today will be old news tomorrow. And tomorrow is a new day when you will get up and enjoy the life you have."

With a bright career ahead of me and looking forward to raising a family, I disliked being told what I could and couldn't do. As I rested from my surgeries, piles of books and magazines with articles about others who had faced similar challenges began to appear on my nightstand.

Some of the people in those stories swore they had experienced a miracle. A miracle would have been nice but they're called miracles for a reason. I needed something more concrete.

Many of the people who defied their prognoses talked about faith and the power of visualization. Envision yourself walking. So when I took a nap, I'd fall asleep making movies of myself walking, teaching, dancing.

I began to say it to everyone. "When I'm up and walking again... " Their faces would go slack for a second as they tried to decide whether I was joking or delusional. My left leg was in a massive cast.

But then they said the right things, encouraging me, telling me how great it was that I believed it would happen, having no idea just how serious and determined I was.

I hoped that repeating something over and over until you believe it would work for me. A wish—to walk again—became a goal. I imagined myself walking and let that be my guide. Even if it turned out that I would in fact never walk normally again, I was training to always think of myself as a person who walks, runs, and dances. I would never think of myself as damaged. Altered, perhaps, but not damaged.

All the emotions associated with trauma and loss rose in me at one time or another—anger, guilt, and despair. One of the concepts that influenced me comes from Viktor E. Frankl's book *Man's Search For Meaning*, an account of his two and a half years in Nazi concentration camps, including six months in Auschwitz where his wife was murdered on arrival.

Frankl had been a neurologist and psychiatrist in Vienna, specializing in suicide prevention. He used what he had learned in his work to keep himself from losing hope in the death camp. He observed the behaviors of others and wrote about it after he was liberated. He wanted to answer the question he was so often asked: Why, in spite of the horrors and the probability that they would die, did he and millions of others not kill themselves to shorten their suffering?

He noticed that even under the worst possible conditions some people were motivated to do good. Starving people shared their food. Others taught languages or music, or kept alive their religious traditions at the risk of being shot. "Those who have a 'why' to live for can bear with almost any 'how'," he wrote.

Since it was first published seven decades ago, millions of people around the world have credited Frankl's book with changing, and often saving, their lives. It confirms for me my belief that by not giving in when we are the weakest, we become our strongest. That's also the message I found in the Bible, especially in 2 Corinthians 12:10 where Paul writes, "I am well content with weaknesses, with insults, with distresses, with persecutions, with difficulties, for Christ's sake; for when I am weak, then I am strong."

Frankl concluded that each of us has the power to determine the purpose, or why, of our lives and that the purpose we choose can evolve over time. In my case, it was to bear witness to God's healing power in my life and the life of others. In Frankl's case, the purpose was to survive the death camp so that he could bear witness against Nazi atrocities.

One of his methods for getting through cold days of digging ditches wearing nothing but prison pajamas was to visualize his wife and talk to her as he worked. He said it helped him to focus on something other than his physical and emotional misery. That's what visualizing myself walking did for me.

As my mobility improved, my doctor and my friends and family began referring to my progress as a miracle. I would say it was a lot of hard work, a lot of praying, and the acknowledgment that, as an African proverb teaches, "When the music changes, so does the dance."

If you think about your life, when the music changes—when things don't quite work out as you thought they would—your best strategy is to adapt. If the tune changes, don't stop dancing. Just change the way you do it.

Viktor Frankl talked to his wife in his imagination to get through Auschwitz. For me, talking to God is one way I deal with life's challenges and I did quite a bit of talking to Him as my knee was healing.

"Okay, God. I believe your Word, and I know a lot of bad things happened to good people in the Bible. I know many men and women were better off after their trials. But I don't know if I can handle this. I want to be better, not bitter. You know me and now you see my condition. You know I need strength from someplace, somehow, to do this."

While I waited for God, I drew strength from my role models. My grandmother had prayed for the butcher when he tried to cheat her with a cheaper cut of meat, but in the meantime she made sure she got what she paid for by demanding it. When all those colleges turned down my applications, my grandmother prayed for an answer but she didn't wait for it, she demanded one and got it.

Those and other experiences had taught me that things are not always as they seem, and that I was responsible for finding out how they really are. This gave me an advantage because I had been quizzing doctors since I was a child. It was understood in our family that physicians are not gods but directed and led by God, and that healing comes from God and from within.

If you take someone else's word that you're not going to heal, or allow yourself to feel defeated, your chances of success are reduced. From the moment I began being treated for my injuries, I chose my doctors as opposed to the other way around. I've never gone to a particular doctor just because somebody said he or she was good.

I've had experiences with a handful of doctors whose bedside manner I found wanting, or who reacted to my questions as though I were interfering. I never went back to see them. In any relationship, whether it's medical, spiritual, or just friendship, there's got to be some trust. Otherwise, I'm going to have trouble being honest.

Growing up black you learn to be wary of people you

don't know, and, subconsciously at least, more so when they are white. The first black teacher I ever had was in twelfth grade. My experience with certain white teachers had given me reasons to be cautious.

Calling my progress a miracle made it all sound so simple, as if I just got lucky when it was really a lot of hard work and the messages I received growing up. I was always strong-willed, which drove my mother crazy sometimes. But I remember her, in a quiet moment, telling me that it was a gift. "You're a strong child. That may work against you sometimes, but you're going to do well in life because you're strong-willed."

After the accident, Leonard was back on his feet in a few weeks. For me it was a good five months before I was able to return to work teaching second grade from a wheelchair. I was good at rolling myself around but the students loved pushing me so I had them draw straws for the privilege.

It took many more months of physical therapy, imagining myself walking, and talking with God, but I did walk normally again.

Seven:
The Heart Breaks
And Melts

One of my all-time favorite books is Charles Dickens' *A Tale of Two Cities*. The long, poetic first sentence begins, "It was the best of times, it was the worst of times ..." and includes the phrase, "it was the spring of hope, it was the winter of despair."

I was newly married to my best friend and doing what I loved most—teaching—but there'd been that accident and the suffering that resulted. It had been the best and worst times of my young life. Also, like Dickens's depiction of the French Revolution, the schools I found myself working in were on the cusp between two cultures in conflict—black and white, have and have-not.

Finally, the novel's overarching theme is about redemption and resurrection. Near the beginning, one of the main characters, who has gone insane, is "recalled to life" by the love of his daughter. The book ends with another character, who has a deservedly guilty conscience, saving a condemned man who is innocent by taking his place at the guillotine. His last thought: "I see a beautiful city and a brilliant people rising from this abyss." In the end, good has triumphed.

One of my other all-time favorites is Maya Angelou's autobiography about her childhood and adolescence, *I Know Why the Caged Bird Sings*, published while I was studying at Pitt. Her depiction of the grandmother who raised her was of a woman much like my grandmother—strong, principled, and resilient. Angelou described how she evolved from feeling like the ugly girl victimized by racism to becoming a confident, intellectually curious young woman able to think and act for herself.

At the time, I was starting to have just that sort of an awakening about who I was and my place in the world. Her book was a confirmation of my experiences and encouragement to keep going, made easier by my love for teaching. Children, especially the very young, are sponges—receptive and eager to learn. In their innocence I have often found occasional flashes of wisdom and insight.

My first assignment was a predominantly white kindergarten class in a school where I was the second black teacher ever hired. Children, like kittens and puppies, are naturally affectionate and my students would often hold my hand. One day, one of the little girls, Melissa, was holding my hand and looking at it intently as she rubbed it.

I was about to ask why when she looked up at me with wide eyes. "You're not dirty!"

I was a little startled, but it was hardly the first time a small child became interested in skin color.

"My mommy said you were dirty."

I took her hand and rubbed it the way she had mine.

"No, I'm not. And neither are you, see? Come on, let's go wash our hands."

At the sink I showed her that the water flowing over my hands stayed as clear as it had when she put her hands under. Then we had a short chat about skin color that I'd like to think she remembers to this day. Hope so, anyway!

One year one of the boys had been given a horn for his birthday that he brought to school and wanted to play during recess. He was very sweet.

"You can play it, Miss Winstead."

The mouthpiece looked a bit grungy and I had no idea how to work the thing anyway, so I suggested that he let some of his classmates have a chance. One of the boys, who was black, was eager to be first but the boy with the horn pulled away and yelped, "NO!"

I intervened as gently as I could. "Why won't you share with the other children?"

"My mother said I can't let any colored kids play my horn."

I stifled a chuckle. "But honey, you asked me to play it."

"You're not colored."

Then I had to stifle a guffaw.

"What do you mean, I'm not colored? Look at my skin. It's just as dark as his. What makes you think I'm not colored?"

"Because you're my teacher."

It was the sort of thing a child will sometimes say that breaks your heart and then melts it, all at the same time. A phrase from Dickens's ironic opening sentence springs to mind: "it was the age of wisdom, it was the age of foolishness." The knowledge that a parent would put such poison in a child's mind was cause for despair. How he processed it was kind of charming.

Another student I once had, Troy, was as dark as me. One parent-teacher night, Troy's mother showed up with Troy in tow. She, Troy, and I—dark as chocolate. His mother and I both had our hair in Afros. She was beelining for me.

"Miss Winstead (I was not yet married), I just had to come meet you!" Her eyes were bright, smiling.

"I'm just glad you came," I said, "but why did you have to meet me?"

She rolled her eyes. "I've asked Troy so many times, 'Don't you have a colored teacher?' And he always says he doesn't. I asked him, 'Don't you have Miss Winstead? Isn't she the black teacher?'" Because I was only the second black teacher in the school, people knew my name.

"Well, he still said no. I asked him, 'Are you sure?' And he said, 'Nope. She's not colored.'"

We burst out laughing.

I sat down in one of the kids' chairs. "Troy, come here." I took his hand in mine. "Tell me, what color am I?"

Suddenly the center of attention, he looked down at the floor for a second. Why was Mommy laughing about him with Miss Winstead?

"I don't know, Miss Winstead."

"Well, tell me this. What color are you, Troy?"

He glanced at his mother. "I'm colored."

"Honey, look at your hand and look at mine. See? I'm colored, too."

He shook his head. "No, you're not."

"Why do you think I'm not? I'm darker than you are."

He shook his head again.

"Oh, no. You're my teacher, Miss Winstead, so you can't be."

The heart breaks and melts.

Perhaps one of the best-known conversations about skin color takes place in James McBride's best-selling memoir, *The Color of Water*, about growing up in black neighborhoods in New York with an African American preacher father and a mother who was born in Eastern Europe to Orthodox Jews. Twice widowed, twice remarried to black preachers, McBride's mother managed to raise a dozen children in the hostile world of New York's black ghettos while working to keep them fed and in school. All her children became successful adults.

McBride wrote that when his mother took the kids out with her to run errands, it always caused a stir. People stared and a few shouted abusive epithets. One day he asked his mother why she didn't look like him and his siblings.

"I'm just light-skinned."

"Am I black or white?"

"You're a human being."

Having married into the church, his mother had converted and the church had been a central part of his family's life.

"Well, what color is God?"

"The color of water."

There have been so many moments like that in my career as an educator. Telling about them now makes them seem even more quaint and touching than they were at the time. In becoming a more equal society, the age of childhood innocence gets shorter and shorter.

In my early years I worked with a principal who believed teachers should switch grades every few years. After kindergarten I taught second grade and had most of the same students again. Then I asked for fourth grade so I'd have them yet again. Then I took graduate school courses to earn a master's degree in counseling at the middle-school level. Then I was working with sixth, seventh, and eighth graders who I had taught in elementary school. By that time I knew most of them and their families.

My students' families became so important that Leonard and I occasionally took into our home a child who was in danger of being homeless, sent into the foster care system, or who just needed a break from an unstable environment. A couple of children lived with us for entire summers and would go with us on vacations and to visit our families. When Leonard graduated from college in 1973, he began his career in an elementary school and together we helped put together and lead youth groups in our church.

Our home became a shelter of sorts that parents and guardians trusted. Although we eventually had two children of our own, we think of ourselves as having another fifteen or twenty who lived with us at one time or another over the years. Many needed help, but we also hosted children just because we liked them.

The first was a boy in my second grade class who was failing. His mother had asked me to pass him anyway so he wouldn't fall behind his classmates and feel marginalized. But he wasn't ready. I convinced her that I needed to keep him with me another year and promised to tutor him over the summer. She accepted our offer to keep him and his older brother with us for part of the summer.

In his first year of teaching Leonard took under his wing another young man, Andre, who lived with his grandmother. Andre and two brothers, Devery and Tony, spent a lot of time with us, going fishing, on picnics, and enjoying the pool at the apartment house where we lived.

Those are wistful memories because that sort of ad-hoc community intervention could never happen today. The law now prohibits a teacher from even giving a child a ride home in her car, let alone hugging and kissing the little ones when they feel vulnerable or afraid or angry. In those days you could love and nurture them as if they were your own, and we did.

We've kept in touch with many of those children over the years. Leonard became a pastor and later officiated at Tony's wedding. Decades since they were our students, they periodically look us up. And when we go out to eat, shop, or to the movies, we still sometimes hear someone exclaim, "Oh, my God. It's Mr. Massie," or "Mrs. Massie," and even as far back as "Miss Winstead."

Years ago I was about to go into a convenience store in a rough-looking neighborhood when I noticed some young men loitering at the door. I decided to go in anyway and as I walked past the men I heard one of them say, "Shh! That's Miss Winstead." I stopped, turned, and looked at him.

"David?!"

"Uh, uh ... yeah. I ... I'm sorry, Miss Winstead. I'm sorry."

"David, you know what? You guys look like a bunch of thugs hanging out here. I was afraid to go in. Turn that hat around right and don't sit in front loitering and intimidating people."

We spoke for a few minutes and as I was saying goodbye he reached out and drew me into a hug. He began to tremble and then sobbed a few times. I patted his back and whispered in his ear, "You were always one of my favorites, David. I'm so happy to see you again."

"I love you, Miss Winstead. You always treated me good. You were the best teacher I ever had. I'm so sorry."

Then he wiped his cheeks and walked out the door.

Driving home, I remembered his broad smile and a wave of sadness broke over me. I never saw him again, but I did pray for him and I hope, if he ever reads this, that he will have found a way to make the most of his life.

More often than not, we hear about former students who went on to successful careers, like the fourth grader who couldn't even read or write his name and now has earned his master's degree in psychology.

When I was a middle-school counselor I was assigned two twelve-year-old girls who were friends. Dee Dee and Sharice skipped classes frequently, were likely using alcohol and drugs, and were hostile and distrustful. They behaved like they were the toughest girls in school. In my eyes they were two young ladies who needed more love and compassion than they were getting.

I ended up just falling in love with those two as I worked with them to shed the negative self-images they had and see their potential. Working with them, seeing what worked and what didn't, helped make me a much better counselor. Years later, after Dee Dee's mother had passed away, she asked me to stand in as her surrogate mother when she got married. She went on to write a book and has earned earn her master's and doctoral degrees.

Leonard and I saw things in certain kids that neither they nor their parents could. Many years later, one young lady whose mother had told her she'd never make it told us, "Even when I tried to push you away, you just wouldn't let me. I thought I just wanted to be left alone because I couldn't see why you would care about me."

Over the course of my career, I developed a style and a philosophy about teaching that was based on knowing more about the whole child and his or her family. You need to know the adults behind the students and what motivates them. It was always important to me to know where the psychological blockages were.

I've had students who fought against me almost an entire school year. Yet those same children were the ones who would cry like babies on the last day of school and try to figure out some way to stay in my class for another year. Those were the ones who would visit me all summer—I used to live in the neighborhoods where I taught—riding their bikes to our house to just sit, have a lemonade, and talk.

Some later wrote me letters about what they learned, which wasn't the math or the English but about who they were as a person or how valuable they were; or that they could make it; or that somebody really cared for and loved them in spite of having been told or made to feel they were unlovable.

Well before I became a mother myself, I had learned a lot about families and it boiled down to this: a child may be said to come from a dysfunctional family but in my experience there are no dysfunctional children. In fact, some of the most functional children I've known came from dysfunctional homes.

Children raised in impoverished circumstances often know a lot of life skills that you can't test for, things most children who live in a loving family with two adults don't have to figure out. Girls being a mother to their younger siblings because mom wasn't around or functioning. Little boys taking on the role of the absent father, having to figure out how to get the food necessary to feed the family.

They learn which streets and which people are safe and which are not; what to do when the electricity's been shut off; how to keep each other warm in winter when the gas is cut off.

Some children are leaders at home, a skill a teacher can build on. Some doodle a lot. That's how they express themselves, through their artistic instincts. Some are talkative and others are listeners who may not appear to be paying attention until you start talking to them and discover they get it but struggle to express it in writing.

I might not have said it this way at the time, but in retrospect what both Leonard and I were trying to do was help children rewrite their personal narratives—to create a personal mythology that was aspirational and hopeful. That process begins with a question that even adults have a difficult time answering: Who am I?

When I became a trainer of teachers, I designed a workshop activity that began with the assignment to write down the answer to that question, which invariably was superficial. I'm a teacher. I'm a principal. I'm a parent. I'm a widow. I'm a caring person.

Then I'd say, "Write it again. Really, who are you?" They'd write something different. I would try and ask that several times, until some of them would be reduced to tears talking about the pain in their pasts, or about who other people think they are versus who they really are.

The point of the exercise was to help teachers deal with their own issues so that they could be more open and compassionate with children. How can you help a child deal with emotional adversity if you haven't dealt with the demons that keep you awake at night?

For Leonard and me, the power of love to heal, to encourage, to instill confidence, to inspire, begins with the love of self. The love of self—belief in our individual possibilities—came for both of us from the love we received from our parents and grandparents. We became teachers because we saw what could be accomplished with a little love applied in the right moments to children who weren't technically ours but who were children of God, in whom rests the ultimate love.

Eight:
Are You My Mother?

"*A*re you really my mother?"

My ten-year-old daughter Michelle and I were sitting at the kitchen table going over a homework assignment to write about her grandparents when she blurted this out. The question struck me as so absurd I instinctively laughed. It was sort of cute, the kind of question children often ask themselves when they discover someone they know was adopted. Was I switched at birth?

"Come on, Shelly. Of course I'm your mother. Who else could be your mother?"

She had such a serious face on. Where was all this coming from?

"You know those pictures of you when you were pregnant with Nicole?" Her older sister was two when Michelle was born. "Well, how come there aren't any pictures of you when you were pregnant with me?"

I felt a wavelet of guilt. By the time Leonard and I

started our family, we had between us more than ten solid years of combined experience with teaching, working, loving, and living with children. When we became parents, we wanted our daughters to feel equally loved and we had the tools and knowledge to raise healthy, caring, well-educated children.

But you can't control for the time you had with your first child alone. It's always going to be there for the children who follow—an awareness that the firstborn had Mommy and Daddy all to herself, until they came along. The second child's birth is as much a miracle as the first. It's just not THE miracle. How to explain?

"Shelly, I probably didn't have a lot of pictures taken when I was pregnant with you because I was so sick during the last three months. I do have pictures, somewhere." I had to think, though. I must have a few, but I couldn't remember where they'd be.

Michelle asked me to tell her again the story of her birth and a string of other questions that made it clear she was looking for evidence to confirm a suspicion that I was not her real mother. That was just the beginning of a decade-long quest that often left me distressed and frustrated. My heart ached from thinking I had failed in some way to show my love for her. Other times her persistent doubt tested my patience.

Soon after our first conversation, my mother phoned to tell me, "I really need to talk to you about something serious." My heart skipped a beat, thinking she was going to deliver some dreadful news.

"What's that?"

"You really need to talk to Michelle about this idea she has that you aren't her mother. I don't know what else to do. I've assured her but she keeps asking me if you are her mother, and would I ever lie to her, and am I telling her the truth. I'm really concerned. I don't know where it's coming from, but she really believes you aren't."

Out came the old photo albums and boxes of unsorted envelopes full of family pictures. I did find some of the day she was born but even after showing them to her, along with a bunch of happy baby pictures, the questioning continued to come up from time to time. When it did, talking about it with her left me feeling deflated.

To grow up emotionally healthy and confident, a child needs to feel safe, and that can't happen if she thinks the most important people in her life are lying to her. With all my experience, it took me too long to grasp the gravity of what was going on in her mind. I had neglected to stop and try to put myself in her shoes. When I did, it all made sense, at least on paper.

Children see and hear more than most adults realize. A child can spin an epic myth out of what adults would consider a snippet of insignificant conversation or a minor anecdote. The myth may be positive. My grandmother's reluctance to talk about the bad old days Down South left a big impression on me. It made her seem more heroic in a way, and set an example of how to deal with adversity—don't dwell on it.

The most innocent comments we make as adults can leave a deep impression on a child's sense of self. I have tried to forgive myself for not noticing or sensing that Michelle was having a real crisis, the seeds of which were planted almost the minute she was born. When I was pregnant with her my sister Mary came to live with us for about a year and a half. She was going back to graduate school and both Leonard and I were working full time.

We offered Mary free room and board in exchange for taking care of Michelle during our work hours. I would take Nicole, our oldest daughter, to daycare and

Michelle would stay at home with Mary. They bonded and it was delightful. Mary had no children so it made me feel good to share the joy of mothering Michelle.

Blended parenting was kind of a tradition when I grew up, both in our family and in black homes generally. For awhile my grandmother had taken in her sister's children. My mother had taken in my father's nieces and nephews. Leonard and I had many unrelated children live with us for periods of time. He and I shared a fluid, inclusive definition of who's family and who's a parent. We didn't adopt any of the children who stayed with us, but we considered ourselves parents and treated them as if they were part of us.

Michelle was born looking so much like Mary, and so little like me, that it became a family joke. "That's Mary's daughter," we sometimes said. Mary would often greet Michelle by saying, "How's my baby doing today?" They were so close I told Mary, "God sent you a baby through Shelly."

When we three were out in public, people who didn't know us sometimes assumed that Michelle was Mary's child. Once we all went to a school play that Nicole was appearing in and got there too late to sit together. One of us would have to sit elsewhere. The usher turned to Mary and said, "How about if you and your daughter sit together?" It happened often enough that Mary and I let it go without comment. It didn't seem like a big deal.

One day Michelle asked me, out of the blue, "Mom, if Aunt Mary ever had a child and couldn't take care of it, would you take it?"

"Of course I would. I would do that for anybody in the family."

When Michelle began expressing her doubts to me, Mary said she had asked her a number of times if she was her mother. Mary had replied, "If I ever had a daughter, I would want her to be exactly like you."

Michelle went off to college eight years later still unconvinced. In her freshman year she called one night as I was walking down the stairs of a restaurant in Washington where I was having dinner. I stopped halfway to answer.

"Hi. It's me. I was just wondering, do you know your blood type?"

"You want to know my blood type, Shelly?"

"Yes."

"Well, I don't know. I think I'm B-positive. Why? What's going on?" I braced for bad news.

"I just wanted to know." She paused. "Mommy, I just want to ask you this one more time, and I really want you to tell me the truth."

I sighed as quietly as I could.

"Sure. Ask me anything, I'll always tell you the truth."

"Are you my mother?"

My eyes flooded and my throat swelled shut. I had to sit down and couldn't speak for a few long moments. What had I done wrong that she still didn't feel a connection? Then we talked.

"Shelly, please tell me. If you don't think I'm your mother, who do you think your father is? Do you think your dad is your father?"

"That's really not important to me. I just want to know. Are you my mother?"

"Sweetheart, Shelly. I don't know how else to say this."

I told her how much I love her. "I must have done something wrong for you not to feel—"

"No. It's not like that. You know, I just want to know."

"Well, if you aren't sure, who do you think your mother is?"

"Aunt Mary."

That's when it hit me, when all the bits and pieces of the story Michelle had created began falling into place.

"Well, we always called Aunt Mary your mother because she doesn't have children and I always felt that God gave me two children so I could share one with my sister. You know how close we are."

She persisted. "No, really ... is Aunt Mary my mother?"

After we hung up I had a wrenching cry. Then I began gathering up the threads. I remembered joking when she was younger, "Yeah, Shelly. Mary's your mother." I never thought much about it. I was kidding. I thought she understood.

Now some other things began to make sense. For example, why, when she became a teenager, she and I went through a rough patch. She was rebellious, impossible to talk with, complained I was too strict, and said she felt I didn't like her. I had chalked it up to typical teenaged behavior. Now I realized it was something much deeper, a kernel of self-doubt that we, as a family, had unwittingly planted and nurtured.

With the benefit of hindsight and experience, I've come to recognize that this question—who am I and where did I really come from—occurs more frequently in black or racially mixed families. What we refer to as the black family comes in all colors and shades. Some generations tend to be light-skinned, some dark. Virtually all so-called African Americans are a blend that can include Native Americans and Europeans, among others.

When Shelly was nearly thirty years old, I was working as an executive with an educational technology company when I had a chance to participate in a training program run by Les Brown, a noted motivational speaker.

One of the people he had invited to join him was actress Cicely Tyson, a heroic, enduring artist and someone I had admired since 1972 when she was nominated for an Academy Award for Best Actress for the role she played in the film *Sounder*. Her character was a school teacher who takes in a boy whose father is serving a sentence for a petty crime, working on a chain gang. *Sounder* was the first serious film about the black experience since *A Raisin In The Sun* and it became a box office success.

I had a chance to speak with her and we hit it off. She told me about a project she was working on, to think of ways to facilitate conversations between mothers and daughters. "Wouldn't it be great," she said, "if we could bring together generations of mothers and daughters and just talk?"

She was preaching to the choir. One thing led to another and we worked together with a film director, setting up interviews that Dr. Tyson conducted with mothers and daughters in my home. The experience was fascinating and emotional for everyone.

There were two interviews that were particularly memorable for me. One was with a mother and daughter where the mother described their relationship as warm, trusting, and loving, but the daughter described it as distant. "My mother and I have lots of issues. We don't communicate."

Her mother listened in stunned silence. As Dr. Tyson delved deeper, the daughter became visibly angry, scolding her mother about the things she'd tried to talk to her about, how her mother cut her off and treated her like a child. "I'm in college now and you don't trust me!"

It was both riveting and hard to watch. "I just didn't know," the mother said. "If you had told me I would have tried to work through this with you. I didn't realize you felt we weren't communicating." In the end, it had been a cathartic experience and they ended up hugging and shedding tears of release.

When it came time for Michelle and me to be interviewed, Dr. Tyson asked a question about our relationship. Although the issue hadn't come up in a long time and we were getting along wonderfully, Michelle mentioned that when she was younger she wasn't sure I was her real mother.

"What do you believe now?" Dr. Tyson asked.

"Oh, I KNOW she's my mother now."

While preparing to write this book, Michelle and I spoke about this part of her life journey. She said that when she was a teenager and we weren't communicating well, her grades were suffering and she felt like she couldn't do anything right no matter how hard she tried. She got so low she even contemplated suicide.

"In spite of having grown up in a church family, it had never occurred to me to pray for guidance," she remembered. "I was young and just so over the whole thing. When it's part of your daily life it can become so routine that you stop paying attention to the words. So I tried to pray. I asked God if He could change things around for me. If He could do that, then I would commit to follow him.

"From that point, my perspective changed. My grades became a little firmer, and my relationships with family got a little better. That marked the first time I made a conscious decision to start practicing my faith, and it was my first encounter with Christ."

Today Michelle is actively involved in her church and her faith is anything but routine.

Nine:

Simply Divine

An acquaintance once asked me to define the role faith has played in my life. "What does it mean when you say your faith has sustained you through your darkest hours? What does that look like? What does that feel like?"

Aside from the specific religious definition—belief in a higher power—faith is defined in dictionaries as "a firm belief in something for which there is no proof," and "complete trust or confidence in someone or something."

Faith, in one form or another, is a universal human need that defies a universal definition. It is intensely personal, shaped by the specific people who have been in our lives, the culture we grew up in, the places we've lived, and the experiences we've had. It's true regardless of religious affiliation. We all want to believe in something bigger than ourselves.

In Hindu and Buddhist belief systems, faith is called dharma. Some dictionaries define it as virtue, or the teaching and doctrine of the Buddha, or sometimes "one's own nature." Dharma refers to the search for life's universal truths and higher purpose. But according to Nitesh Gor, author of *The Dharma of Capitalism*, a book on business ethics, "Ask a million Hindus what dharma is and you'll get a million answers."

The seeds of my Christian faith include having the good fortune to be born into a wonderful, supportive, and passionate church family. A great-grandfather had been a preacher in South Carolina, before our family moved Up South. My grandfather and great-uncle had founded a church—Morning Star Baptist—in our corner of West Mifflin, Pennsylvania, close to Pittsburgh. The initial officers and leaders were my grandmother, her sister, and their husbands. They were the keepers of the flame when I came along, with my grandmother the most vigilant and active of all. From the time we could read, my sisters, my brother, and I each had our own Bible, well-thumbed and smudged from daily use.

As a family, we spent so much time at that church it was really an extension of our home. Morning Star Baptist Church was the beating heart of our family as well as of the black community in the Whitaker Projects. The congregation was small when I was young. Perhaps 150 parishioners attended Sunday services. When I became a choir girl, sitting between hymns and waiting for the next cue, my mind would wander. One day, looking out at all the raised faces watching, listening, nodding, raising their hands as the preacher spoke, I realized that most of them were my relatives. I counted them up—about half the folks in the pews!

That part of western Pennsylvania, downwind of

Lake Erie, gets a lot of snow. Occasionally there'd be a Sunday when a blizzard raged and the snow was so deep and the air so cold that no one showed up—except for my grandmother, my grandfather, my aunts and uncles, my cousins, my parents, my siblings and me. We never missed a Sunday because of weather. That was one manifestation of faith that left a strong impression on me. The message was clear: in our family, faith was not a hobby or an optional convenience. It defined our lives and drove the family narrative.

So Morning Star was thought of as "our" church, or more specifically my grandmother's. Fear of God's judgment in Heaven can be an effective deterrent for mischief-makers, but nothing made the kids and young adults in that community tremble more than the thought of facing my grandmother's judgment here on earth. If you saw somebody messing around like they shouldn't, people would say, "Better not let Miss Cartledge catch you doing that!"

I joke about the fear my grandmother could strike in someone she thought needed guidance, but it wasn't really fear, it was a rare kind of respect, earned honestly. In her case, she earned it by prevailing against all the trials and tribulations she had seen and lived with Down South and the ones she found when she moved Up South. She earned it by turning what could have been hate into love. She lived her faith day in and day out with dignity, compassion, and fierce determination. When confronted with injustice, she responded like the proverbial firefighter who runs into a burning building when everyone else is running away.

Miss Cartledge, also known affectionately as Nina, was the woman who padlocked herself to a rental agent's radiator to get her house painted. She was the person who gave my second grade teacher a verbal spanking for treating me like some cartoon pickaninny. She was a busy and vocal leader who spread the word of God everywhere she went, whether you thought you needed it or not. She could scold the butcher for trying to cheat her on a cut of meat and then turn it into a Bible lesson in front of a store full of white women. I'm sure that butcher remembered her words the next time he had the urge to shortchange a customer.

Nina lived her faith by always going out to visit the sick and the homebound. For a time she baked buttery rolls that we kids would help make and deliver to her customers, and some given for free to those in need. When we were elementary school age, she took us along to help with chores like cleaning and cooking. Later, we all took turns chauffeuring her to her visits and doing the food shopping for herself and those who couldn't do it themselves.

For much of my youth, Morning Star served as a social hall where my friends and I could get together away from the pressures of being black in a school that was practically all white. My crowd consisted of a dozen girls who had formed a social club. Our football team was the Vikings, so we called ourselves the Del Vikings—very Motown. Everybody had to have a nickname—Breezy, Stoodie, Tito, Sleepy, and me, Peaches, or sometimes Pete. If some of us decided to get together at church for choir rehearsal, every one of the Del Vikings would show up.

My mother—Miss Barbara Jean—directed the choir. Between her and my grandmother, once you were in the choir there was no turning back. My mother taught me (made me, at first) to lead songs, something I turned out to enjoy and be good at. I have been doing it ever since in many different settings. Music is an important part of my life. It has played a central role in my family and has been a way for me to express my faith.

When the choir required discipline, my mother treated all the kids equally. She never hesitated to yell at me when she thought I deserved it, and the same with my friends—equal justice. She would not hesitate to alert some errant child's mother that her son or daughter was horsing around at practice or getting sassy. She—we all—understood that the poor child faced another dose of discipline at home.

One level up the hierarchy, if Miss Barbara Jean happened to mention your behavior to her mother, Miss Cartledge, you were probably going to have to do some time. "Time" was the hardest punishment of all—you weren't allowed to go off and play with your friends. When we became teenagers, doing time included being grounded for parties, the teenager's equivalent of life without parole. It was excruciating to be stuck at home on a Saturday, watching the clock hands sweep away the minutes, knowing all your friends were out dancing the night away.

An important step in developing one's faith at Morning Star involved publicly professing your belief and the ritual of baptism by water. Public profession meant you had made a personal commitment—witnessed by your community—to choose right over wrong, to live as closely as possible by the teachings of Jesus. Every Sunday in Baptist churches there is a "call to discipleship," sometimes referred to as "opening the doors of the church." That's when the preacher asks if there is anyone who is ready to take the Lord into his or her heart. "Is there anyone here who wants to make that declaration today?"

The preacher would wait patiently for an answer, for what sometimes seemed like an eternity. It made you think. "Uh-oh! Is he waiting on me to come up? Does somebody know that I did something bad or I broke a rule, and they want me to come up and ask God's forgiveness?"

Those who were ready would rise, walk up the aisle, and stand in front of the whole congregation. Everybody would clap and call out words of encouragement, and then you made your profession of faith. One Sunday when the preacher had "opened the doors," my close friend Tito, sitting next to me, leaned over and whispered, "I dare you to do it. A quarter says you don't have the nerve."

The easiest way to get me to do something was to make it a dare. I immediately turned to Aldine, sitting on my other side, and whispered, "If I go up there, I dare you to go with me. A quarter says you haven't the nerve." Then I stood up and walked down the aisle to the front, my friends following close behind and wondering what had just happened.

The congregation erupted with tears of joy and praising the Lord. It was something to see the beaming looks of love and hope on all those faces. Today I can appreciate what they were witnessing—three adorable girls on the threshold of young adulthood, in our best Sunday dresses, making our professions together as friends. They might not have been so moved had they known it started with a dare.

I had seen enough of these moments to know that I was expected to declare my belief that Jesus died for our sins, commit to living the Word, and acknowledge that I needed His help to do it. That was the easy part. It was only afterward that it began to dawn on me just how profound this act was for my family. My grand-mother went on and on about how wonderful it was, how I was turning my life around, and that it was time I was baptized.

Baptized? I'd never thought much about it. I didn't know how to swim. Dip my whole body under the water? That sounded like drowning. But the die was cast. I had won fifty cents, enough for a matinee at the Leona Theater in Homestead, and there was no un-professing your faith.

Morning Star lacked its own baptismal pool so the next Sunday a bunch of my friends went with me to Second Baptist Church where we all got baptized. Nobody wanted to be left out. A more powerful child-hood bonding experience is hard to imagine. My baptism was the true beginning of my comprehension of faith.

Setting aside cultural and familial religious traditions and practices, there is some universality in all people, whether they believe in God, Allah, follow the Buddha, or don't believe in anybody. A child born in a religious vacuum is still going to grow up with a set of values and beliefs shaped by family and community—a form of faith. Someone might say, "I don't believe in anything," but they will also say they have guiding principles around which they design their lives.

Faith is a belief that there is a design for our lives, whether we think we know what it is or not, and regard-less of what we think it should be. About five years ago I started having vision and memory problems that turned out to be caused by a non-malignant tumor underneath my brain. The symptoms were caused by the tumor pressing on nerves. In the process of searching for a specialist surgeon I could trust, I met Dr. Kofi Boahene at Johns Hopkins University Hospital in Baltimore. He had grown up in Ghana and made his way to the States where he'd become an innovator in finding new ways to remove such tumors without having to crack open skulls.

His kind smile and gentle confidence put me at ease but I had to ask, "Do you believe in God? Because I do." If I was going to choose a doctor to poke around inside my head, I preferred one who might get a helping hand from the Almighty.

"Oh, yes," he said, grinning. "Like you, I do believe in God. But that's not the question. The question is, Do you *know* Him?"

We bonded. I had faith that our meeting was part of God's design, and the surgery was successful, leaving my skull intact.

Like I did, Dr. Boahene grew up in a deeply religious home but in Ghana in West Africa. His father was a missionary. His family prayed together every day and studied the Bible together. When he was just about to go off to study medicine in Sweden with a full scholarship, his spot was given to someone else. Instead he was sent to the Soviet Union to veterinary school. He had no interest in animal medicine but hoped that once he got there he could persuade his advisors to let him switch.

The day he was to leave Ghana's capital city of Accra for Moscow, his first time leaving his home country, he was glum as he rode in the car with his family to the airport. From what he'd read and heard, Russia was a gray, unhappy land and inhospitable for Africans. Now he was going to spend four years there learning a skill he had no interest or intentions to use. He wanted to help people.

His grandmother saw the solemn look on his young face. What she said to him that day sustained him through a long and improbable journey that led from Russia to the Mayo Clinic and then to the best hospital in the US, Johns Hopkins.

"Don't be dejected by what has happened," his grandmother said. "What God has designed for you, nobody can take away."

Twenty-five years later, Dr. Boahene says his grandmother helped refine for him what faith means. "God had a plan for me but He wasn't ready to share it. Faith is the assurance of things hoped for and the conviction of things not seen. Although my profession is based in science, I believe in the power of faith."

Another surgeon, one of Dr. Boahene's closest colleagues, tells the story of his mother's death that illustrates the idea that the true source of healing is in the unknowable. Dr. Ife Sofola's mother was in the final stages of liver failure. Dr. Sofola, born of Nigerian parents, was a decorated US Navy flight surgeon working at Bethesda Naval Hospital. He arranged for his mother to spend her last days there so she could be among her closest relatives. She slipped into a coma with a Do Not Resuscitate order, reserved for patients who cannot be saved.

The family was heartbroken. Without consulting the family, his distraught sister arranged to have a traditional tribal healer flown all the way from Nigeria. She kept it a secret until the healer walked in to their mother's hospital room.

"I was dismayed," Dr. Sofola recalled. "But there was nothing to lose so my siblings and I let him stay. The healer instructed us to hold hands in a circle around my mother's bed and pray."

They had been praying in silence for just a few minutes when the healer abruptly announced, "It is done," and left to take a taxi back to the airport.

"It was a relief that he wasn't going to launch into

some long-winded or undignified ceremony that might have upset everyone," Dr. Sofola says. "I thought, Well that's it, then. Twenty minutes later, my mother woke up, smiled, greeted us all, got out of bed, and took a shower. I was utterly dumbstruck. My heart was overflowing with joy and I dashed out into the hallway to announce, shouting, 'A miracle has occurred! Here, at Bethesda! A MIRACLE!'"

Dr. Sofola's mother left the hospital and spent precious days with her children and grandchildren at home, saying goodbye. Her explanation for the sudden recovery? "I came back so you would have faith." She died peacefully a few weeks later.

Dr. Sofola thought about how many hours he'd spent in lecture halls, how many books he had studied, how many operations he had performed, and concluded, "We are doctors so therefore we think we know something about life and death. In fact, I wonder sometimes if we know anything at all."

When life serves up a rough patch or a tragedy or some other challenge, people who are struggling with their faith sometimes get the idea that God is punishing them and they wonder why. We all have our Job-like moments when we start to feel like God is testing us unfairly. I've had lots of them and when I say that my faith sustained me, I mean that I looked to God's Word for comfort and accepted that God's plan for my life is a mystery. Leonard, who has been a leader and preacher, calls it divine design. A colloquial way of saying it is that everything happens for a reason.

Faith is the belief that even when you've been in a horrible accident on your honeymoon and don't know if you'll ever be able to walk normally again, it's part of God's design and—the most important element—

it's designed for you to learn something that will make you stronger. If you're in a bad season, a sad season, a dry season of life, and things are going wrong one after another, I've had to learn to ask, "Lord, what am I supposed to learn? And please help me learn it fast so I can get out of this season."

True faith or spirituality means giving up on the idea that you are a victim. God is not punishing you. He is giving you a challenge, and it's up to you how you choose to deal with that challenge.

Faith means always aspiring to a high level of personal behavior, to be more like Jesus Christ in our compassion and in how we cope with suffering. Church and faith have been such an integral part of African American life because it's what sustained the culture through centuries of unspeakable cruelty and marginalization.

Contrary to what some non-African Americans think, African slaves did not have to borrow European religious traditions to know God. The worship tradition in African societies—call and response, music and dancing—is ancient. Christianity has been part of the African landscape from the beginning.

My generation came of age at the end of the era when black parents told their children, "It is what it is. You're black and there are some privileges and protections you're just not going to have and you need to accept it." African American culture was maturing and faith was growing during the civil rights movement until we faced our greatest test—the murder of Reverend Dr. Martin Luther King Jr..

I was in high school when it happened, on April 4, 1968. That was a low point for us and everyone we knew. What happened, we asked ourselves, to the part about the righteous being exalted by God? Dr. King was a man of strong faith. His example—fearlessly pursuing equality in spite of the risks—was an inspiration. His cold-blooded murder was a test.

It took faith to accept that God called Dr. King home early for a reason, and then to find the lessons in such terrible circumstances. African Americans have had a lot of experience with turmoil and it was during the worst times that our faith as a culture grew fastest and became strongest. Faith has been our most powerful tool for surviving the indignities of slavery and all the misery that has flowed from it.

Martin Luther King spoke about his faith in the language of justice. His example became the driving force for African Americans who face, on a regular basis, all forms of injustice. You didn't get the job, your high school guidance counselor lied about your grades to sabotage your college goals, you didn't get a raise you deserved—faith allows us to talk about and process our feelings in the context of God's mysterious plan.

Finally, for me at least, faith has been about noticing and reaching out to those who are, as the Bible says, "least among us." In a church, that means anyone who walks through the door is not only welcomed, but also embraced and encouraged to have an encounter with Christ.

Every now and then a person we don't know will show up who looks a little lost or just doesn't fit in. I might not notice them until someone sitting near me whispers, "Oh, look at that woman in the back there. She's dressed like a prostitute!" On occasion someone will show up reeking of alcohol so bad you could just about see the fumes.

They often sneak in to church after the service has started. It might be a woman who wobbles in wearing stilettos, a tube top, and a skirt that barely covers her behind. In that case I'll find a spare jacket or long scarf and offer it to her: "This might make you feel more comfortable." There's no need to explain, chastise, or criticize. They came to church—God sent them to us—in need of comfort.

These latecomers, who feel out of place, will try to slink out the door after the service. I know about that move and I catch them if I can. Then I'll try to get them to sit and chat.

"Can we talk? Would you sit down with me for a few minutes? How are you feeling? What's going on with you? I noticed you came in late. Are things okay?"

This one says she's drowning trying to raise six kids. That one's had an addiction relapse. Another is bewildered by the death of a spouse. Those are opportunities to make a big difference in someone's life with the smallest of gestures. Sometimes I'll give a person a few dollars and sometimes a few hundred. Sometimes I get them in touch with social services they might need but don't know about.

Always I'll send them off with a hug. Sometimes, as I put my arms around them, they begin weeping. It may be the first time they've ever been embraced and felt the power of God's love.

So the answer to the question that started off this chapter is this: Faith is comfort. Faith at its most manifest is in the giving of comfort.

Part III
The Power Of Persistence

Ten:

It Only Looks Easy

*F*ollowing the example of my parents and grandparents, I've avoided dwelling on the hard times and taught our daughters Nicole and Michelle to "take a day to cry" when they encounter a setback or a disappointment, then pick themselves up and keep going. This has sometimes given others the impression that we haven't had much in the way of hard times, that it's been all sunshine and roses.

"You know, I wish my life was as easy as yours," a visitor once said during a chat at our suburban home.

It was such a misguided notion I laughed. "A nice house doesn't mean I haven't been through my share of things. I've been through plenty."

From time to time our daughters have passed on similar comments they've heard, usually some variation of, "Well, you wouldn't understand. You've had it easy."

When I hear these remarks, I'm unsure whether to

feel proud or chastened. On the one hand, we apparently succeeded in setting an example and raising children who don't whine every time things don't go their way, or cling to their hurts. On the other hand, people who haven't known us that well apparently thought our family had life so completely figured out that we couldn't relate to those who were troubled, in distress, or struggling with health issues.

The genesis of this book was in that gap between perception and reality, especially as it relates to health. There was the car accident on our honeymoon. Twenty years later I started having trouble with the knee that was shattered and I had to go through a series of painful procedures and an implant to be able to walk normally again.

In the space of about nine years I had to have my gall bladder removed, a hysterectomy that included removing a massive tumor, a lumpectomy, treatment for pericarditis (fluid around the heart) and pleurisy (irritation of the lining of the lungs), and I had a tumor removed from under my brain. After all that, Leonard was treated for prostate cancer, kidney disease, and now a bone marrow disorder. So much for the easy life!

After I began having my litany of physical problems I was invited to do some public speaking before diverse audiences. I've spoken about what's gotten me through it all—family, faith, love. People came up to me after and said things like, "Wow, I can't believe what you've been through. You don't sound like it. You don't look like it. I don't know if I could be so together about it all." Not at all what I expected.

Until I began sharing my story I thought everybody's life was like mine, that everyone experiences disarray and trauma in life. Now I can relate to something Mother Teresa once said: "I know God will not give me anything

I can't handle. I just wish that He didn't trust me so much."

With all that I've experienced, one of the hardest things God gave me to handle was the end of my career as a public educator. I started out teaching second grade in Baltimore County in 1971. Thirty-two years later, I was appointed interim superintendent of the Washington, DC, schools and it appeared I was in line for the appointment to be permanent. In between I had many good years, but it wasn't a straight line and it wasn't easy, even when it looked that way.

After four years of classroom teaching and earning a master's degree from Johns Hopkins University, I was promoted to human relations/guidance counselor in a junior high school, responsible for developing and leading a new program of individual and group counseling for students as well as staff. My superiors said they saw potential in me and encouraged me to make staff development and training a central focus of my career.

As part of the program, I counseled students and also designed and facilitated workshops for parents, students, and faculty. The goal was to find ways to work with families, not just the students. As a teacher, my class assignments had allowed me to teach the same students for several years. I got to know many of their families and saw firsthand what a big difference it could make in a student's achievement to have parents and other relatives engaged. We worked with parents on how to help with homework, how to maintain healthy relationships, and to understand the intense changes that middle-schoolers go through.

It was exciting work because nothing like that program had existed in the Baltimore County Schools. The administration had picked that particular middle school to develop it because it was in a neighborhood that had been predominantly white and was becoming desegregated. There was a great deal of friction among the students, staff, parents, and community. New, inclusive techniques were needed.

Roughly a decade after I moved on from classroom teaching, I had become the personnel director of the same district, which surrounds but does not include the city of Baltimore. It stretches from the poorest neighborhoods bordering the city in the south, along the industrial shoreline of the inner harbor, to the rolling farmland and sprawling horse estates of the wealthy in the north. To get from one end to the other is an hour's drive. With nearly 100,000 students and roughly 7,000 classroom staff, it was a big job with lots of responsibilities and opportunities.

By any measure I had come a long way—a second grader from the Jects standing up for herself against a teacher's ignorance; the young adult denied an essay prize she'd won; the young woman denied the honor of high school homecoming queen after she'd been elected; the college bound student whose dreams were sabotaged by her school counselor; the happy bride whose marriage began with a devastating injury. God had given me a lot to handle but in retrospect, He was just getting started.

My mantra, take a day to cry, proved insufficient when, in 1987, Leonard and I separated and then divorced. He had been unhappy in the marriage and had broken his vows. It came as a complete shock and I was emotionally shattered. We ended up with joint custody of our daughters, who were in elementary school, and agreed to joint counseling. I wanted to be sure that the girls distinguished his relationship with me from his relationship with them. Leonard loved them dearly and they loved him.

Since we would have to come face-to-face with each other when dropping off and picking up our children, counseling gave us an escape valve. It was where we could hash things out so we would be less likely to exchange harsh words or display negative feelings in front of the children. I wanted them to see their father and mother getting along peaceably, even though the sessions were so upsetting that I lived in dread of every appointment and walked out of many before they were over. Had I not been a counselor myself, I would have thought it a waste of time, but I knew I had to do the work.

It was sometimes hard just to hear Leonard speak, hard to hear what the counselor was trying to say, and I felt excruciating pain when we walked out the door after our sessions and he went to his car and I to mine. I had grown up with this man. We had been best friends. We had survived our honeymoon accident. We had played mom and dad by providing a temporary home and guidance to so many children. It had taken us six years to become pregnant and have our first child, Nicole, and then Michelle two years later.

We had been constant champions of each other's careers. Now he had suddenly become a complete stranger and the bottom dropped out of my self-confidence.

Counseling was like living a soap opera, one hour per episode, one episode per week. The problem was that lots of things happened to each of us between the episodes so we couldn't simply pick up where we left off. It would have been impossible to continue without our shared faith in God that this suffering was somehow part of His plan, for *both* of us.

Faith, hope, optimism—whatever word you use, it seems humans are programmed to redefine and create feelings of happiness in unhappy situations. In a TED Talk video, "The Surprising Science of Happiness," Harvard professor Daniel T. Gilbert talked about studying how people define happiness before and after a major catastrophe, and after a stroke of phenomenal luck. At one extreme, a seventy-eight-year-old man who had served thirty-seven years in jail for a crime he didn't commit told reporters his incarceration had been a "glorious" experience. "There were some nice guys there. They had a gym."

Gilbert calls this "synthesizing happiness." We have a survival instinct to make the best of what we have, and a tendency not to agonize over what we cannot have. Like Moreese Bickham—the innocent prisoner—I could look back after the fact and think about what I learned and accomplished during this time. But when it was happening, I was filling up God's voicemail box every day.

At one point Leonard revealed that he had been praying that God would pull our family back together. I, on the other hand, was praying that God would show me how to deal with this tragedy and remain a good mother through it all. We shared one central goal—to raise our daughters feeling part of a nuclear—if split-atom—family. We wanted them to feel loved equally by both parents.

We agreed and stuck to never speaking negatively about each other around the children. We would collaborate to ensure that they did well in school, conducted themselves with dignity and propriety in their social lives, and received a solid basis in Godly living. Figuring it out on that basis helped us change our behaviors and get back to a more civil and compassionate relationship. Repairing the marriage was not on my agenda.

In spite of my aching heart, my busy professional life, and my responsibilities as a parent, I began working on my doctorate in education administration at the University of Maryland. I had my cry and it was time to get busy and think about the future.

On class nights, I'd pick the girls up from school, feed them a quick dinner or snack, and take them with me. I'd find empty seats in the classroom and set them up to do their homework. Their treat for enduring my hectic schedule was a stop for pizza on the way home.

Gradually, over a period of several years, Leonard and I began to break it down—the reasons we broke up, what I needed and what I didn't want in a relationship, what I missed about being married to Leonard, and what I didn't. Likewise for him. I grew to accept the separation and began to move forward with less baggage and less mistrust.

I could not change my circumstances, but I could change the way I was dealing with them and find some joy in my life. In the words of Viktor E. Frankl, the Auschwitz survivor who wrote *Man's Search For Meaning*, "Everything can be taken from a man but one thing: the last of the human freedoms—to choose one's attitude in any given set of circumstances, to choose one's own way."

The greatest challenge was getting past my anger. Somehow, after four years divorced and a great deal of praying and soul-searching, we managed to get to the point that we agreed to remarry. However, I still harbored some hurt and it surfaced now and again. One night we were arguing about something at dinner and Nicole piped up, "Why did you even get back together?"

"Because your father is my best friend," I blurted. I meant it and they knew it was true, but it may have sounded a little less convincing than before the divorce.

A few years after, Nicole was a student at Vanderbilt

University in Nashville, Tennessee, when she fell madly in love. They dated for a while and then the young man abruptly dumped her. Her heart was broken and she sank into a deep depression. She stopped attending classes, lost her appetite, and laid in bed all day with the lights out, crying. I called her every day. "How are you doing today? What did you eat? Are you moving on?" It was the sort of crisis that gives parents their worst nightmares about the midnight phone calls they pray they will never get.

One night Nicole couldn't get a word out, she was crying so hard.

"I'll call you back in a little bit," I said. I immediately made reservations for Leonard and me to fly down the next day. I called Nicole back. "We're coming tomorrow. You just hold on. And eat something. I booked a room at the hotel across from campus. Come and meet us there."

She showed up, still crying uncontrollably, and spent the day with her head in my lap, weeping, while I held her saying, over and over, "It's going to be okay." She needed permission to grieve. By evening she had finally exhausted most of her tears. Then I made it clear she did not have permission to give in to her misery.

"When you're going through Hell, don't stop to take pictures, remember? Now," I said, "what are we going to do about this? I feel your pain, and I understand it. But where are you going to go from here? What does your life look like?"

Nicole survived her broken heart, as I had mine. I kept busy with my career and the distractions of life and family. I refused to dwell on the past. If you had asked me at the time, I would have said I had so much to be grateful for and that made me feel happy.

About ten years after Leonard and I remarried, I was

feeling exhausted and worn out by work. I n
give myself a few days away to restore my ene
sort some things out. Nicole had heard about a
center in western North Carolina called Well of _____.
It had recently been started by two women who were
members of the Sisters of Mercy, a well-known international network of charities. The brochure described it
as a "quiet sanctuary for adults in need of a temporary
respite from daily demands, expectations, and stresses or
those who may simply wish to move apart for a time of
prayer, rest, and renewal."

It sounded like just the ticket. Nicole volunteered to
drive me there. It was an opportunity for us to spend an
extended time together, just the two of us, away from
home. I packed my clothes in one bag and put it in the
backseat along with my briefcase, computer, work documents, and BlackBerry.

We arrived to find a setting even more beautiful
and forested than the pictures, the quiet broken only
by singing birds and running water. That part of North
Carolina seems to have streams everywhere, all carrying
runoff from the Great Smoky Mountains all the way
to the sea. It was the perfect place to get some real,
undistracted work done.

As I got out of the car Nicole grabbed my briefcase
and walked to the back of her car. She opened the trunk,
put my briefcase in, and slammed the lid—clunk!

"Wait! What are you doing? I need my briefcase. It
has all my stuff in it."

"You won't need it." She flashed a mischievous grin.

"How will I call you without my phone?"

"You won't."

"But ... I'll get bored." I could see where this was
going, but I suddenly felt off balance.

"You won't be bored, Mom."

"But... well ... at least I need my phone. What if there was an emergency?"

"If there is, we'll call the office and they'll know where to find you."

"So ... what'll I do then?"

Nicole came over, took me by the hand, and said, "Talk to God. He'll speak to you if you talk to Him. All you have to do is listen. Okay? Love you, Mom! Relax!"

She gave me a warm hug and then off she drove, leaving me standing there thunderstruck, wondering what I was going to do to keep from climbing the walls. Wasting time swinging in a hammock was never my style.

There were only eight other people staying there that week. It was the quietest place I had ever been. I walked around the grounds and trails for two days in silence, just smiling and nodding to the other guests but fighting the urge to strike up conversations.

I got my first Reiki massage, walked the labyrinth, sang by myself in the chapel, and even chose a private "quiet table" for meals, discovering it was sometimes nice not having to make small talk. I began to feel proud of being able to do even that simple thing—come to a beautiful place and listen to the silence.

I kept a notepad with me the whole time, in case God wanted to speak to me, but even He was silent. So I had written about the beauty of the Well of Mercy, the good organic food, and the need for everyone to get a Sabbath—a time of rest and restoration.

On the last night, before the morning Nicole was returning to pick me up, I was in my small dorm-like room, lying on the bed, listening to the sounds of the forest creatures as I drifted off to sleep. It had been a truly restful break and I looked forward to returning home refreshed and ready to resume conquering the world.

In the middle of the night, my eyes popped open. I awoke fully alert. Out of the clear blue, God spoke to me. "Forgive him." I grabbed my notebook and sat up in bed, writing it down. "Forgive him." Then I added a question mark.

Forgive who? I had gone to Well of Mercy expecting to sort out some career issues. What's with this forgiveness message? I was baffled. Who? My father, my boss, my friend for not repaying that loan?

Then God said, "It's the only way you will heal and be whole again. You have to forgive him."

Who is "him"? I began to write down the names of every "him" that had ever hurt me. With each name I wrote, my feelings of anger or resentment intensified. The last name I wrote was Leonard's. I stared at it as if it had been written by someone else. Then I began to cry and my heaving became uncontrollable sobs. Why? Hadn't I forgiven him for the big thing as well as all the small things?

His voice said, "No, you haven't. Stop carrying this burden around. Stop hurting yourself. Stop hurting him. If you don't forgive him, how do you expect to be forgiven by Me?"

I spent the next few hours crying and writing. I was trying to figure out why I had to apologize when it was his fault, not mine!

Then came the revelation. God reminded me of the things I had done and had failed to do that contributed to our break-up. He showed me the man I married in 1972. He showed me his heart—not the former heart, but the new heart. He revealed to me that I wasn't the only one hurt. So was Leonard. The truth left me overwhelmed with shame. I cried on and off until first light.

Then I dressed, packed my bag, and sat quietly at breakfast feeling awful about myself.

I was sitting outside on a bench when Nicole pulled into the driveway and the car came to a stop. I quietly put my bag in the backseat and got into the car. She looked at me expectantly.

"Well, Mom. How was it?"

I could barely speak and she seemed to understand that I needed that silence, so I kept my thoughts to myself on the ride to her house. When Leonard came to pick me up, I slid into the passenger seat feeling a mix of grief and relief.

"So," he said, flashing his signature warm smile. "How was the retreat?"

Tears flooded my eyes and the words wouldn't come forth at first. When I was able to, I said I realized that I had not fully forgiven him when we remarried. I had never let some things go. In spite of all the many things he had done over the years to show me that he had changed and regretted his past decisions, I had not truly believed him. In fact, I had decided I could never trust him, or anyone else, as I had in the past.

And then I told him about that night, the revelation about feeling I had dealt with and released past hurts.

"Leonard, I'm truly sorry. I'm asking for your forgiveness for all the hurt I have caused you."

It was Leonard's turn to cry. "Elfreda, I have been waiting ten years for this moment. I forgive you, too."

The Well of Mercy had lived up to its name and Nicole had revealed her uncommon wisdom. God, I decided, must have spoken to her first.

In the years that have followed, I have from time to time spoken to groups at my church and elsewhere about how to deal with relationship problems. I break it down as follows, based on experience and lots of observation.

1. Go through it, not around it. The most difficult part of dealing with a broken relationship is to accept that a change has taken place and things are not going to be the same. You have to grieve in order to move on. Eventually, the intensity of the pain will lessen and you will be able to experience joy again. While dealing with the loss you can gain increased awareness of yourself, what is important to you, and what are your needs and your strengths.

2. Detach and revel in your independence. Avoid rushing into another relationship or trying to win the other person back. Avoid getting into a physical relationship that may make you feel loved but doesn't really fill the gap. It's better to go ahead and eat that quart of ice cream! Remind yourself that you were made whole and you don't need another person to complete you or to make you happy. With the help of God, you will fill the emptiness.

3. Shift your focus to others and away from yourself. When I'm in pain, I remember that someone else is worse off and mine is minor by comparison. Focus on giving to others. When I feel empty, I become full by giving what I have and forgetting about myself. That has gotten me through some very tough days.

4. Laugh a lot and cry a little. Both are healing. Neurology Professor William H. Frey II of the University of Minnesota, an expert on Alzheimer's disease and pharmaceuticals, headed a team of researchers who found that emotional tears (not

the tears that come when you get dust in your eyes or chop an onion) contain toxic biochemical byproducts, and that crying releases toxins and relieves emotional stress.

5. Work it out. Find something productive to do. Be active. Learn a new skill. Getting my PhD during the divorce filled my sleepless nights with reading, writing, and conducting research. It wasn't much fun, but the prize was worth it. I spent time with friends and family, but the focus of my life was getting that degree as quickly as possible. Work out your grief and pain by exercising, walking, swimming, playing tennis—keeping your body active. Try something totally new and different. Program yourself to be too busy to think about your loss.

6. Make new friends, keep the old. A relationship breakdown will reveal your true friends. They can help you get through it, but resist the urge to reveal the private details. Take the high road and speak only in general terms about your feelings and not about your lost partner. Friends are not your personal advisors. They have not walked in your shoes. At the same time, create a new circle of friends who have no history with your ex. Many of the new friends I made were women and men who had been in similar situations and were in various states of recovery.

7. Don't shut love out—love again! Once our hearts are broken by a failed relationship, we tend to close off pieces of our heart so no one will be able to get inside and hurt us again. That was God's message to me at Well of Mercy. Noted Dutch

author and priest Henri Nouwen once wrote, "The more you have loved and have allowed yourself to suffer because of your love, the more you will be able to let your heart grow wider and deeper."

8. Forgive. It's magical, as I discovered. Matthew 18:23-35 teaches that if we do not forgive others, God will not forgive us of our wrongdoings to others. Forgiveness means letting go of bitter feelings, resentment, and vengefulness. Negative feelings eat away at you on the inside. Holding grudges can lead to physical and emotional illness. Forgiveness is necessary to move on and it can lead to increased empathy and new, healthier relationships.

Eleven:

Nothing But My Undies

*I*f you've ever had one of those dreams in which you find yourself in a public place and suddenly realize you have nothing on but your underwear (or less), you have an idea of what my professional life felt like in 1999. It was a nightmare, except it was real and I was wide awake.

For more than twenty years my work in public education had steadily become more interesting, complex, and rewarding. I started out teaching and, after four years in the classroom, was recruited into a program that led to successive promotions in staff development and training.

During that period I had risen through the ranks to become director of personnel services for the Baltimore County Public Schools, the twenty-fifth largest school district in the country. Along the way I had earned my master's degree from Johns Hopkins University and my doctorate from the University of Maryland, where I codesigned and taught a course in human relations.

In 1991 I accepted an appointment as associate super-intendent of personnel in the Montgomery County Public Schools, seventeenth largest in the US and largest in Maryland. With well over 100,000 students, the district stretches from the wealthy border suburbs of Washington, DC, in the south to the hinterlands of farm and horse country an hour north.

For the next five years I led a number of system-wide recruiting, training, and professional development projects in close coordination with the board of educa-tion. As a member of the district's leadership team and executive staff, I worked directly with Dr. Paul L. Vance, Montgomery County's first black superintendent. He had been promoted from within the same year I was hired.

Dr. Vance was a national pioneer among black school administrators and became a beloved mentor to me. The son of a sanitation worker in Philadelphia, he'd earned his undergraduate degree at Cheyney University, a histor-ically black college, in 1952 and then started his career as a teacher in the Philadelphia Public Schools.

Later he became a principal, serving during a period of intense racial strife in urban districts across the country that were under court order to implement desegregation plans. To do so required busing black students into white neighborhoods, and vice versa. Public education became a battleground in many communities.

After earning his doctorate from the University of Pennsylvania, Dr. Vance had gone to work for the Baltimore City Public Schools, rising to deputy superin-tendent before joining the Montgomery County system in 1977 as an associate superintendent. There he'd worked his way up to the top job during the transition from a largely white student population to about 40 percent black, Asian, or Hispanic.

Dr. Vance, who'd been on the frontlines of history his whole career, was known for exhorting his teachers and administrators to avoid labeling children as "minority" students. Speaking to a group of principals in 1991, the *Washington Post* reported, "He said that he had a 'bitter' resistance to the characterization 'minority' and 'minority students' because it sets them aside, it makes them something special.

"It puts them outside the mainstream. It implies that there is something mystical or magical that can be done to light the sparkle in their eyes and make them more productive learners. The term 'minority students' perpetuates barriers against children."

We agreed about that and on setting high expectations for all students—not just the lowest- and highest-achievers. He took me under his wing and helped me learn the ropes of how a large, racially diverse district is run from the top down. He made it clear he had high expectations for me and his confidence motivated me to fulfill them.

Dr. Vance was a generation older than me and well liked. To truly follow in his footsteps, I would have to make a lateral move to another district where there were opportunities to advance. Such an opportunity presented itself in 1996 when I was offered the second-highest position—deputy superintendent—of my former school district, the Baltimore County Public Schools. My new superintendent was Dr. Anthony G. Marchione, a first-generation Italian-American who'd grown up in Baltimore.

In the five years I had been away from Baltimore County, the district had become a lightning rod for controversy. Dr. Marchione, like myself, had worked his way up from the classroom and had just been appointed superintendent after serving on an interim basis. The previous superintendent had been fired.

In a system with an enrollment that was growing progressively more African American, race and the performance of schools in poorer neighborhoods was a central issue. Dr. Marchione was chosen over other candidates in part because he was deliberative and measured in his approach, whereas the school board considered his predecessor a bit too outspoken and provocative.

In the process of reorganizing the district's top administration, I became Baltimore County's first black deputy superintendent. In my new role I supervised five area superintendents and oversaw all of the schools, instructional offices, personnel operations, staff development, and community/government relations. I told a reporter from the local newspaper, "This feels like home. I was here for twenty years before I went to Montgomery County."

The news appeared in the *Baltimore Sun* on April 10, 1996, and I immediately found myself caught in the crossfire of a political skirmish.

> For some black leaders, the move signifies an effort by Dr. Marchione to smooth conflicts with the county National Association for the Advancement of Colored People and other African American organizations, who vehemently opposed his appointment.
>
> "It sends a positive signal that there needs to be diversity in not only how we educate students but for those we hire to educate children," said board member Dunbar Brooks. "At that level you influence the climate of the school system and ultimately what happens in the classroom."
>
> Asked whether he hoped her appointment would help soothe race relations, Dr. Marchione said:

"I've always had a commitment to having a balanced superintendent staff."

But if anyone hopes Dr. Massie's appointment will help Dr. Marchione's relationship with county NAACP official Bernetha George, signs are it won't work.

"Bringing on black faces does not resolve the problem," said Dr. George, vice president and education committee chairman of the county branch of the NAACP. "Black faces have always been in the Baltimore County school system, and the problem has thrived," she said, referring to the persistent achievement gap between black and white students.

A week later, one of the paper's columnists wrote a follow-up piece headlined "Real Education Issues Under Racial Cloud." It was even more unsettling.

Say a little prayer for Elfreda W. Massie, blameless until everyone discovered she was black. Then, many things happened all at once. She was named deputy superintendent of Baltimore County public schools. White people went: Wink, wink, we know what that's all about. Black people went: We know what it's all about, too, and don't try to patronize us.

And poor Dr. Massie doesn't even show up for work until July.

When Dr. Anthony Marchione named Massie his No. 2 person last week, it followed considerable hand-wringing over Marchione's own recent appointment. The NAACP, pointing to continuing gaps between black and white kids' classroom performance, wanted a black superintendent. Some whites felt the National Association for the Advancement of Colored People was unfairly blaming Marchione, the interim chief, for generations of perceived white insensitivity in schools.

So, when Marchione reached down to Montgomery County for the unknown Massie, it set off a new round of talk about racial sensitivities. Clearly, Marchione was making a peace offering. Clearly, nobody bought it.

And poor Massie's own impressive background— a master's in education from the Johns Hopkins University, a Ph.D. in philosophy from Maryland and then important jobs in the Baltimore and Montgomery county school systems—seems virtually ignored in the current atmosphere.

Thus do we wind ourselves more tightly in the suffocating grip of racial gamesmanship, wherein whites in power offer symbolic gestures and blacks seeking power see through it, and the kids in classrooms continue to flounder and nobody has an answer for this.

Somehow, "poor Dr. Massie" survived the next two-plus years and received good marks for my performance as steward of a billion-dollar operating budget.

About the time I started my new job in Baltimore County in July 1996, my former boss, Dr. Vance, announced that he would be retiring at the end of his contract in 1999. He had been having some unexplained light-headedness and was driving his car one day in 1995 when he lost consciousness and had an accident. It happened again in 1996 and although medical tests failed to find the cause, he had to give up driving at the age of sixty-five. (In spite of his condition, Dr. Vance would actively live another eighteen years!)

Early in 1999, I got the call that changed my life in ways I could not possibly have imagined. Dr. Vance wanted me to succeed him as superintendent of the Montgomery County schools. I would have to compete with other candidates, but just being asked was a huge honor and I knew that if he was on my side I'd have a fair chance of being invited to interview.

The vetting process was long, complex, and thorough. Because I thought it might make a difference, I told Dr. Vance and two members of the board of education who were encouraging me to apply that there were two things in my background they ought to know about. The first was the four-year gap in my marriage to Leonard, which ended when we remarried in 1992. No one batted an eyelash over that.

The second was our personal bankruptcy filing in June 1998, a record year with more than 1.4 million personal bankruptcy petitions in the US. Banks had been pushing credit cards like crazy and millions of people had discovered how convenient it was to use them for everyday expenses as well as emergencies.

It was easy to just make the minimum payment and overlook the growing balance—until you started bumping up against your credit limit. We had spent many thousands of dollars helping family and friends and one day realized our incomes could not support our debts. We consulted experts and were advised to file for bankruptcy protection.

Most of what we owed was in the form of mortgages. One was on our home and the other was a rental property. We used the bankruptcy law to rearrange our finances so that our unsecured creditors would get paid. It was embarrassing for a top school administrator to have to confess to poor money management. Knowing the political nature of a superintendency, I was prepared for the board to find it a disqualification.

But no one I mentioned it to seemed to think it was a deal breaker. Several decision-makers assured me it was the sort of thing that had nothing to do with my job and "could happen to anybody."

On Friday, April 30, 1999, the Montgomery County board issued a press release announcing that I was the finalist for the job. It was a red-letter day and I wasted no time telling family and friends. A photographer for the *Washington Post* came out to shoot a portrait to run with the news story. The press release made it official.

> The Board of Education of Montgomery County has narrowed its field of candidates for superintendent of schools and identified Dr. Elfreda W. Massie, deputy superintendent of the Baltimore County Public Schools, as a finalist who will meet with community, civic, government, business, parent, student, and education leaders next week in interviews designed to help the Board make its final selection and appointment.

> "The meetings with leaders of key constituency groups are considered important steps in helping the Board of Education determine the best possible candidate to lead the Montgomery County Public Schools into the next century," said Mr. Reginald Felton, president of the Board of Education. The Board is planning to make its final decision in May.

> The Board widened the selection process in order to allow major stakeholders an opportunity to meet a finalist for the position of superintendent

in a series of small interview sessions designed to permit a frank and open exchange and dialogue. The interviews will be held Friday, May 7, as a continuation of the Board's selection proceeding.

The Board identified Dr. Massie as a finalist after narrowing the list of possible candidates from among those who best matched a "leadership profile assessment" derived from public forums and a survey about the qualities necessary in the next superintendent of schools.

It was the culmination of a quarter-century of hard work and preparation, and a singular honor to be following in the footsteps of my mentor. That Saturday—a beautiful, sunny spring day—I celebrated with Leonard, our daughters, and a house full of other relatives, friends, and members of our church who stopped by to offer their congratulations.

I went to bed Saturday night exhilarated and looking forward to church the next morning. There would be more validation and prayers of thanksgiving. I put a little extra thought into my outfit and sang in the car as Leonard drove and I looked out the window at the lush countryside and blooming gardens—all seemed right with the world.

But when I got to church, the faces who greeted me were all wearing worried looks.

A friend sidled up and whispered, "Elfreda, have you seen this?" She handed me an envelope with a document inside. It was copy of our bankruptcy court records. "Everybody in church got one."

I was confused at first. It made no sense. But then I read the cover letter written by one of the trustees of our church—the church Leonard was pastoring—questioning my fitness for the superintendent's job because of the bankruptcy.

It was the most humiliating church service I ever sat through, knowing everyone was thinking the same thing—"poor Dr. Massie." I hadn't felt that embarrassed since high school when those three women from the Daughters of the American Revolution discovered I was black and refused to give me the essay award I'd won.

Worse yet, I discovered that the same documents had been sent to every member of the Montgomery County board of education, as well as the local newspapers in Washington, DC, and Baltimore. By Monday morning I'd received word that my appointment was in jeopardy and the phone started to ring off the hook with calls from reporters. An article in the *Washington Post* the next morning made it official.

Massie Filed For Bankruptcy

May 4, 1999: The Montgomery County Board of Education suspended its consideration of the front-running candidate for school superintendent yesterday, hours after learning that she and her husband filed for personal bankruptcy protection last June.

The revelations threw into confusion Montgomery County's search for a successor to Paul L. Vance, whose term as head of the 128,000-student school system, second-largest in the state, expires in June. Officials had expressed strong satisfaction last week with Massie as the lone finalist put forward after a four-month nationwide search.

But late yesterday, school board President Reginald M. Felton released a statement saying that "in light of the seriousness of these allegations, I have suspended any further proceedings of the candidacy of Dr. Massie as superintendent until a complete and thorough explanation can be provided to the Board of Education."

The executive search firm for Montgomery County said it conducted a criminal background check on Massie and found nothing but did not look into her personal finances. The firm also conducted a review of how Massie handled finances in her job. A spokesman said, "When we checked in terms of how she managed money in the [school] district, she was impeccable."

School board members expressed shock and concern at the revelations, but at least one said Massie's candidacy was not necessarily doomed, depending on the circumstances in which the debts were incurred.

Massie, who was to be in Montgomery this week for meetings and interviews, said that she was not withdrawing her candidacy and that she still believed that she would make a good superintendent.

"While I understand concerns that people may have about my having filed for bankruptcy," she said, "I can say that it has not and will not interfere with my ability to lead Montgomery County public schools forward."

The next day's *Baltimore Sun* ran an article that helped ease the pain a little but could not undo the damage that had been done. The headline read "Colleagues Praise Deputy Superintendent: Many say bankruptcy shouldn't affect her bid for Montgomery position."

"It should be a nonissue as far as I'm concerned," said Baltimore County Superintendent Anthony G.

Marchione, who hired Massie from Montgomery County schools in 1996. "She will be an outstanding superintendent someplace, someday, whether it's in Montgomery County or elsewhere."

Marchione said that he learned of Massie's financial troubles shortly after the June bankruptcy filing, through an anonymous letter. He said he discussed it with Massie, and then "dismissed it."

"The reality is that her personal financial situation has had no relation to what she's done on the job," Marchione said. "She has had responsibility for department and office budgets, and there's never been any problems whatsoever."

Baltimore County school board President Dunbar Brooks said Massie's bankruptcy filing does not affect his confidence in her.

"I'd just say for the record that I have the highest trust in her integrity and competence," he said.

Other school officials and board members said they were unaware of the financial problems until news reports yesterday. And Ella White Campbell, a community activist along the Liberty Road corridor, though "shocked" at word of Massie's problems, praised her skills in working effectively with neighborhood groups.

"She has been very instrumental in reestablishing confidence in the school system in the minority community. She has taken decisive action, and she has done it very quietly and diplomatically," Campbell said.

In the past year, several Baltimore County school board members have discussed Massie as a likely successor to Marchione if he retires in 2000 as expected. She also has been mentioned as a potential replacement for Howard County Superintendent Michael E. Hickey when his contract expires in 2000.

All the praise in the world couldn't un-ring the tolling bell. It was clear the Montgomery County board would not entertain my application in a second go-round and face a political ruckus. To keep my hat in the ring would just prolong my misery. So I met with the Montgomery County board that night and let them know I was withdrawing my name from consideration.

In my official letter I wrote, "I don't believe in any way that my personal financial circumstances impede my ability to serve in a position as superintendent, nor do they affect my skills and competency to do the job."

In a matter of two days I had gone from the peak of my career into a valley of despair. Then it got worse. The next day, May 6, a front-page article in the *Wall Street Journal* mentioned my name in the context of a vote by the US House of Representatives to "crack down on Americans who use the personal-bankruptcy system to shirk debts they could afford to pay."

> Actor Burt Reynolds and former baseball commissioner Bowie Kuhn have wiped out debts through bankruptcy. And reform advocates are circulating the bankruptcy petition of Elfreda Massie, who was a leading candidate to become superintendent of the Montgomery County, Md., school system when the *Washington Post* reported her filing on its front page.

A week later, just seven days after I thought I had reason to celebrate the most important milestone of any educator's career, let alone a black woman in a world dominated by white men, the *Washington Post*'s personal-finance columnist wrote a piece that helped put things in some context. Michelle Singletary's column struck a deep chord in me as well as many other black women who grew up in modest circumstances and became pioneers in their chosen fields.

Singletary knew what she was talking about. She is a black woman who became a nationally syndicated columnist, author, and Oprah Winfrey favorite. She achieved enormous success in the news business, another institution long dominated by white men. Like me, she grew up in a poor black neighborhood (in Baltimore) and the person who most inspired her was her hard-working grandmother, Big Mama.

> Last week, a candidate for Montgomery County school superintendent withdrew her application after it was revealed that she had filed for personal bankruptcy. School board members seemed to be rankled that Elfreda W. Massie hadn't disclosed this matter to them during the interview process.
>
> Never mind that there is no indication that Massie ever misused any public funds while serving as deputy superintendent in Baltimore County. The revelation derailed her candidacy.
>
> As I read the news stories, I could just hear my grandmother fussing about the whole affair. She had a strict policy against revealing any of her own personal financial information, even to family members.
>
> "Ain't nobody's business what I do with my money," Big Mama would say.
>
> For me, the Massie case illustrates a troubling trend. Do we want employers to routinely hire,

promote and fire people based on how they manage their private funds? If that were the case, I know there would be a lot of good workers unemployed.

Basically, my grandmother was right on the money. It's nobody's business but your own how you manage your own funds. Certainly not your boss's.

Among Michelle Singletary's readers, I'm sure there were more than a few public officials in government and education—especially the black ones—nodding their heads in recognition. It's hard to judge a black pioneer in certain professions by the same rules as a white person. It reminds us of that well-worn cliche in African American culture about the hundred-yard race where the white person gets to start halfway to the finish line. This message is pounded into the heads of many black children who go on to successful careers and professions: You have to be twice as good to get half what you deserve.

I was one of those black children and I learned from a very early age how true it was then. We've come a long way since, but in 1999—before a black man had been elected president—I knew that my personal financial woes had touched the third rail of negative racial stereotypes. Like my high school guidance counselor who deliberately sabotaged my college applications, I knew that, subconsciously at least, many white people reading about my troubles would be more suspicious of me because of the color of my skin.

Nowhere else have these deep-seated cultural differences flared up more often and openly than in public education in districts with diverse populations. The civil rights movement, federal legislation, and major court decisions have made public education a fertile profession for black people. As a culture, we know good schools and teachers make all the difference in how our children turn out.

The comments made in those articles about my losing the superintendency reflect the intense racial politics that have festered for years in many districts with diverse populations. Where board of education members are elected, candidates run and caucus based on race. One election cycle, the board may have a majority of white members who fire some black administrators and give those jobs to white candidates, including friends, relations, and political allies—patronage jobs.

The next cycle, the black community is so outraged that white folks are running a black school district, they turn out in droves and replace the white majority with a black majority. The new board fires the white people and replaces them with black candidates. And on and on it goes.

I have tried my best to forgive the person who whacked that hornet's nest, but I have wondered what unseen political forces might have been at work. It had been such a personal and calculated tactic.

Now I was living the nightmare that ends with you out in public in your undies. Just going to the supermarket meant bracing myself for the possibility of running into someone familiar and having an awkward moment.

In the days and weeks that followed my public fall from grace, my philosophy—take a day to cry then get back up and keep going—was hard to live up to. The topic was in the press for a week or so, and many articles mentioned my name. A *New York Times* writer used our story to illustrate what one social scientist called "luxury fever" that turns people into "spendthrifts." Another article that mentioned us ran under the headline "Congress Aims to Stop Affluent From Dodging Debts."

Affluent? Who were they talking about? Our household income was about $175,000 a year. We had two mortgages, two daughters going through college and beginning their careers, my father-in-law needing costly eldercare, and all the other usual and unexpected expenses that always seem to crop up. It was hard to read those articles without shedding a few tears of frustration, shame, sorrow for the effect on family and friends, and grief at what was lost.

One moment it had been a beautiful sunny spring day and the next I was falling into a dark, bottomless pit.

Twelve:

I Can't See!

*T*he celebration that had brought together my family and friends became more of a wake.

Everyone assured me that, "God has a plan. There's a reason for this. Remember David and Goliath. You'll get through it. You'll be fine." The unconditional love helped. So did duty. As an educator and community leader I was obliged to set a positive, dignified example. I might be dying on the inside but I still had my active role at church and my responsibilities as Baltimore County deputy superintendent. I did my best to put "it" in a box so I could focus on what mattered.

Dying inside is an exaggeration, but not by much. I had missed the train of life and found myself standing on the platform watching what I wanted and almost had get smaller and smaller until it disappeared.

The complete loss of privacy made it many times worse. In my quiet moments, with tears and prayer, I pondered. Now what?

An answer came in January 2000, about eight months after withdrawing as a candidate for the Montgomery County superintendency. An executive recruiter approached me with an offer to join an educational publishing company—Rigby Education—headquartered near Chicago. Rigby, which produced literary and training resources for educators, needed someone with experience at the superintendent level to become their vice president for professional development.

Training was my specialty, the position paid well, and it was at the executive level. It was a chance to realize my dream of having a second career in the private sector that would have a positive impact on public education.

The job required moving away from all things familiar, a challenge but also an opportunity to experiment with a fresh start. I liked the idea of lots of travel, visiting school districts, interacting with peers, and building a professional network. I decided to take the plunge.

For the first six months I lived in Illinois and Leonard shuttled between Chicago and Maryland. The commute soon proved exhausting so we agreed that if he could find a job as a principal in Illinois, he would consider moving. He interviewed for three positions and was offered all three. He saw it as a sign it was time for him to join me.

Giving up his position as the pastor of Resurrection Baptist Church was a major sacrifice. My family was "leaning in" with me long before it became fashionable.

Three years later we had successfully resettled, I was enjoying the work, and we were getting back on track financially—and then the company threw me a curve ball. The Chicago offices were relocating to Austin, Texas. I couldn't ask Leonard to go through another upheaval.

The company assured me I could commute and still do the job, but I doubted I could be as effective. We decided to come back to the East Coast.

While I'd been away, Dr. Vance, my mentor and superintendent of the Montgomery County schools, had a brief retirement of about a year before he was back in the saddle. This time he was head of the District of Columbia Public Schools, which was in a deep crisis. The mayor called it a "slow-moving train wreck."

Enrollment had been declining as public charter schools gained popularity and families of school-age children moved to the suburbs. Reading levels had scraped bottom, there was evidence of financial misman- agement, and incidents of violence were increasing. As in many other urban areas, dropout rates were high. Some of the buildings needed such major repairs that it was going to be cheaper to tear them down and rebuild.

The district had been unable to keep a superinten- dent longer than two years. The DC Financial Control Board had coaxed Dr. Vance, then seventy years old, out of retirement in 2000, hoping he would be a stabilizing influence until a new superintendent could be found.

We had remained good friends and I often sought his counsel. When I told him our plan to return, he imme- diately asked me to be his chief of staff, a job I would not have considered under any other circumstances. I wanted to avoid stirring things up and I expected our bankruptcy—my scarlet letter—would disqualify me.

"I'm not that interested," I told him. "But since it's you asking, I'll interview and if I end up being the best candidate, fine."

My financial history turned out to be immaterial in Washington so I was once again my mentor's right-hand person, running a major school district. Leonard found a position as an elementary school principal in Northeast Washington and we were back doing what we had done for so many years in the Maryland schools.

Just five months later, in November 2003, came another curve ball. Dr. Vance called a press conference one afternoon and announced—to the shock of everyone, including me—that he was resigning. He made a public statement expressing frustration with the political infighting, deficits, and all the other endless crises.

"There's going to be a great deal of confusion and politics," Dr. Vance told the *Washington Star*. He was seventy-three years old by that time and sounding justifiably worn out. "I just don't want to be bothered with it all."

He left the building immediately following the press conference and I was called into the conference room where the board rebounded by offering me his job, effectively immediately. I'm sure to them it made perfect sense, but it happened so fast, in the space of a few hours, that my head was spinning. There was no time to think it through, to ponder and to pray.

Warning bells were ringing in my head. I had been here before. It might burnish my professional record to be superintendent of a highly visible school district. But first I'd have to survive another toxic political environment.

I stepped back from the brink. I told the board I would consider serving only on an interim basis, only until a permanent replacement could be recruited. Being asked to hold the fort and encouraged to apply for the permanent position was enough of a public vote of confidence. Maybe, I thought, the last word on poor Dr. Massie will not be the Montgomery County fiasco but the endorsement of the District of Columbia.

Although I was filling in, there still a press gauntlet to run. A week after Dr. Vance resigned, the *Washington Post* published a long profile that was mostly hopeful and gratifying. The good stuff was at the top and the scarlet letter was mentioned but not dwelt upon.

It still made me jumpy to see my name in print. The article ran in a prominent position on the front page of the local news section under the headline, "Suddenly in the Spotlight at D.C. Schools." I read bracing for the worst.

> Elfreda W. Massie is something of a mystery to many District officials. Since arriving five months ago to take the job of school system chief of staff, she has kept a low profile and rarely spoken to the news media.
>
> "I really don't know her," said Kevin P. Chavous, who heads the D.C. Council's education committee. "She's been very low key."
>
> Massie will have the difficult task of trying to improve a deeply troubled school district as a temporary appointee. But people who have worked with Massie ... describe her as a strong manager who knows what needs to be done to improve student achievement.
>
> "She's extraordinarily competent," said Nancy S. Grasmick, Maryland's state superintendent of schools. "She's extremely organized. She doesn't recoil from difficult decisions."
>
> [Anthony J. Marchione, her former boss in Baltimore County, said] "She has a personal style ... that is intuitive—knowing when to be a good listener, when to be assertive."

Not so bad, I thought. When I finally got a chance to speak with Dr. Vance a few weeks later, he admitted hoodwinking me into the on-deck circle. He knew that if he had tipped his hand up front—that he wanted me to work for him and then have his job permanently—I wouldn't have applied.

He had queued me up by creating a crisis and endorsing my appointment. But I did not want the job. I knew a lot of my time would be spent on politics and dealing with a city in the transition. There would be precious little time for me to work on instructional issues and on improving student performance—the true business of education.

Dr. Vance was crestfallen. "Elfreda, I can't believe you aren't staying. It was all set up for you. You were the perfect person, and I knew they would want you." But he understood my reasons.

After just a month or so as interim superintendent, I was hearing from recruiters looking for candidates for jobs with educational consulting, communications, and publishing firms. I had told the school board from the start that if the right opportunity came along I was going to take it. I worried that the process of replacing me could be dragged out. Some board members tried to persuade me to stay, but I was determined to leave on my terms and timeline. I gave notice and finished my last day near the end of April 2004.

For most of the next five or so years I was a marketing executive with a company that provided large-scale emergency notification and parental outreach solutions. I joined a team of creative, energetic entrepreneurs and that became one of the best jobs of my career.

I enjoyed the camaraderie of meeting new people and learning about their lives and work. I spent a lot of time traveling—my great passion—for business and for pleasure. For four summers I traveled with a group of musicians and singers appearing at jazz festivals in Spain and France. I got to hear, in person and up close, some legendary performers like B.B. King; to be inspired by new cultures, food, and people; and to experience what it's like to be a black person in other societies.

Travel relaxes me. I'm freed of the expectations that come with familiarity. I can be just another face in the crowd. I don't have to behave as expected or feel like I have to be the strong one in a group. I can talk to people and be as anonymous as I choose.

Travel took my mind off myself, but that began to change in 2006. My left leg, the one that was so badly damaged in the honeymoon accident, had been giving me trouble for a long time. I'd been advised to have the knee replaced with an implant, but I kept putting it off because of work. There never seemed to be an opening when I'd be able to take off a month or two for recovery.

When the discomfort got bad enough, I went in for the knee replacement. The surgery is not very complicated and the success rate is high. But I had what can only be described as a worst possible nightmare, the kind that gives you the willies just thinking about it. My surgery went off without a hitch, except for one thing—a pump that supplied the painkiller to my knee *fell out,* and no one noticed.

I was under anesthesia, so I was immobilized and couldn't speak. But I could hear the saw grinding through bone and I could feel the pain. There is no way to exaggerate the hideousness of that torture.

In the recovery room, when I regained my ability to speak, I was hysterical. A nurse checked the pump and discovered the disconnection. Then the outrage began.

The hospital dodged responsibility. The surgeons said the pump could have fallen out after the surgery. But the nursing staff told my family it must have fallen out in the operating room. The details I recalled were too accurate and they could see just how excruciating the pain was.

In the following days I slowly got over that trauma and the new knee was working well. The doctor said it could last me twenty years. It was a relief to have *that* behind me.

Soon after, I started having a different sort of pain that was diagnosed as a rare disorder of the sympathetic nervous system, regional complex pain syndrome. Known by its acronym, RSD is a by-product of traumatic limb surgery. It causes continuous, intense pain that worsens over time, and mine did just that.

I slowly got over that trauma but this situation was still not behind me. My knee would spontaneously freeze at an angle. I couldn't straighten or bend my left leg. Physical therapy couldn't loosen the joint so I had a second surgery. That didn't work either.

When I had recovered enough to begin rehabilitation I was told the recommended regimen called for two sessions with a physical therapist each week. I figured if two was good, logic suggested that more would be better. I signed up for five times a week. Healing was my full-time job until I could get back to my full-time job!

My physical therapist had to scold me at times. "This is too often. You need to rest a little bit." And I would. There were also times when the challenge of pushing a little harder kept me going.

"If you can't fly then run," Dr. Martin Luther King Jr. once said. "If you can't run then walk, if you can't walk then crawl, but whatever you do you have to keep moving forward." That was what I learned growing up and the application of that lesson has rarely let me down.

During one of my check-ins, the doctor tried to rein in my hopes.

"Elfreda, I've done everything I can do for you, but I'm not going to get this knee to bend any farther. This is it."

"I'm ready to push," I said.

"If I work any harder, I may re-break it."

"Well, we're in a hospital, aren't we? If you break it, just wheel me right up to the emergency room and we'll get it fixed."

"Do you really want to take that chance?"

"There's a little more give in there. I can feel it."

It turned out I was right, although to get that knee bent was so painful I needed shots to block some of the nerves. Once we got the knee bending, the doctor again tried to temper my expectations.

"You're not going to be able to walk normally again," he said. "You'll walk with a limp for the rest of your life. It will take a lot of time for your body to adjust to the knee, and for the knee to adjust to the body." There was more: a high risk of reappearing scar tissue that could require additional surgery.

Next stop was an RSD specialist who sent me to the Rubin Institute for Advanced Orthopedics at Sinai Hospital in Baltimore. For all its woes as a city, Baltimore benefits from being a hub of medical research. Thanks to the influence of Johns Hopkins, consistently ranked at or near the top of all hospitals globally, group specialist practices have sprung up around it. The Rubin Institute is devoted to the treatment and study of bone-related problems in the back, arms, legs, and feet. They get people up and walking and help them stay there.

The Rubin enrolled me in an advanced physical therapy program where I found myself among other wheelchair-bound adults and some children with severe orthopedic and neuromuscular conditions. One of the other patients with RSD was a woman in her early twenties who looked so deflated and defeated I was moved to reach out and try to encourage her.

She talked often of her young children who missed her when she came from Pennsylvania to Baltimore for her weekly therapy. During one conversation, tears ran down her cheeks as she said, "The doctors say that seventy percent of people who have RSD aren't ever going to walk."

My knee was in worse shape than hers, but I replied, "I've heard. I'm in the thirty percent that will recover."

Her eyebrows bunched up. "Well, I don't know how you're going to do that."

I gestured toward the children in the room who were diligently working with their therapists to stand and walk.

"Look at those little children. Many of them were born struggling to live normal lives. They've never known anything else and they are fighting to overcome their limitations.

"Here we are, two grown women, and you're telling me what percentage can't do something? We're in the can-do percentage, just like the kids. If they can work as hard as they are, we can work harder."

She persisted with her dismal self-prognosis until I finally said, "Girl, you better get busy and figure out how to get out of that chair! You have things to do and a family to raise." Of course, it's never that easy.

My mobility gradually improved, no more surgery was required, and I eventually could walk normally again. People began referring to my progress as another miracle. That's not how it felt. I had my moments of feeling demoralized and sorely tested.

What got me through was celebrating the blessings in my life, things we take for granted like being able to get out of bed, smelling flowers, sitting in the sunshine, being part of a loving family, and countless other gifts from God.

Back on my feet and back to work, I was looking forward to attending a conference that was being held in Hawaii, a place I hadn't been, when I developed severe intestinal discomfort that turned out to be a gall bladder attack. The surgery required to remove it was scheduled just a few days before I was to leave. Leonard, our daughters, my mother, my sisters—everyone in the family—tried to convince me not to go, but I was determined.

"Who knows when I'll have another chance to go to Hawaii? Besides, I made a commitment and I can't back out at the last minute."

"If you're going to go," Mary said, "someone should go with you, just in case." I didn't think I'd need help but I agreed to take her with me. Two days after I was released from the hospital, we boarded the plane for the twelve-hour flight to Honolulu. By the time we touched down, I was feeling miserable and grateful for Mary's company and help.

As soon as we got into the hotel room I crawled under the covers and fell into a deep sleep. Mary tried to rouse me for dinner but I had no appetite and no energy for dressing or going out in public. She brought me some rice, which I picked at and then fell back to sleep.

The next morning, when it was time for me to do my first presentation, I dragged myself out of bed, splashed some water on my face, put on lipstick and mascara, and went into battle. As soon as I was done, I went right back to the room and fell asleep again.

I was on several panels and made it to all of them the same way—marshaling my strength long enough to get up, do my job, and then right back to bed. As for beautiful, exotic Hawaii, I saw what I could from the back seat of taxis and from the hotel room window.

I fully recovered from the surgery and the travel,

but in the months that followed I started having other problems. It began with my eyesight. One morning I woke up with pain and blurred vision in my left eye. Both my eyes were so sensitive to normal daylight I couldn't keep them open. I laid back down and after a couple of hours felt better.

When it happened a second time I went to see my ophthalmologist, who diagnosed it as iritis, an inflammation of the iris. She put some drops in my eyes, gave me a prescription, and told me to contact her if it happened again. She seemed unconcerned and the problem appeared to have resolved itself.

About a week later I was getting settled in my seat on a plane at Dulles Airport, about to leave on a trip, when the passenger beside me opened the window shade. The sudden burst of light was accompanied by a sharp stabbing pain in my left eye.

I cried out and instinctively clapped a hand over it to block the light. I had my eyes shut so tight I couldn't see out of the right one either. I asked the passenger next to me to hail a cabin attendant. Her voice was at my side in an instant.

"What's happened?"

It was if I had been thrown into a closet without warning and the door slammed shut—a suffocating, terrifying sort of darkness. My voice quivered with panic.

"I don't know! Something must have happened to my eye. It hurts something awful and I can't see. I can't open my eyes!"

Thirteen:
Where Am I?

A n object of some sort must have flown into my eye. I couldn't imagine what else could have caused such sudden, sharp, and intense pain. It took my breath away and made me dizzy.

My first thought was to get off that plane, no matter what. The door had closed but we hadn't been pushed back yet. That was a blessing. At least we weren't 30,000 feet up in the air.

The cabin attendants opened the door and escorted me off the plane. I protected my eyes with my hands as best I could. Back in the terminal with my eyes closed against the light I fished in my handbag for my phone. When I opened it the light was blinding. I handed it to a ticket agent and asked her to call the person who'd brought me to the airport, a friend who ran a car service.

The driver had mentioned that she was picking someone up at the same terminal a little later. I was sure she was somewhere close, another blessing. At least I was near to home and could get help fast, not blind and stranded in an unfamiliar city. She answered on the second ring. Thank God!

"Please come get me. I need to go to the doctor right now. Something crazy is going on with me. I don't know why, but I can't see."

An hour later I was sitting in an exam chair in a pitch black room in my ophthalmologist's office. It was a relief to be able to open my eyes, even if it was to be swallowed up by total, inky darkness. Once I had calmed down, the doctor came in and applied some drops for pain that took the edge off.

"Elfreda, I think something else is going on," she said in a tight voice. "Something other than just iritis. Have you gotten checked for anything else? Is there anything else you can think of?"

My balance had recently been a little off. It seemed like I was having to say "Excuse me!" a lot from bumping into people. Someone in my family had pointed out that I had developed a slight limp. At first it didn't seem like a big enough deal to see a specialist. After all the surgeries that had been performed on my left knee, plus the effects of time, something was bound to wear out.

Whatever it was, it wasn't enough to slow me down. I was fine otherwise. In any case, I was in my prime career years, enjoying my work and its rewards. I had no time to stop for another knee operation followed by months of rehabilitation.

Now that I wasn't fine otherwise, doctor appointments began to sprout like weeds in my already overgrown calendar. A neurologist speculated that it might be multiple sclerosis. I knew people who had MS and were living a full life. I could handle that.

Then I spent hours on the Internet reading up on the subject and doubts crept in. When I prayed about it, nothing clicked—I never heard the Lord reply, "Yep. That's it. You'll be fine." The neurologist confirmed my doubt.

The next possibility mentioned was lupus, or some other impairment of my immune system. If you are a medical professional you may already suspect where this diagnosis is headed. The reason the specialists did not at the time is that I failed to tell them about my eyes. It was an episodic problem. I'd have an attack, need a day or two to recover, and then I'd be okay for a spell. In any case, what would an eye problem have to do with a limp? So it never came up.

While the neurologist and the immunologist continued testing me and searching for clues, the time between vision spells shrunk. Around Easter 2010, I got off a plane in North Carolina on my way to the wedding of our daughter Nicole. She picked me up in her car and at one point as she turned a corner it happened again, just as swift and painful.

"AAAAH! Nicole! I can't see!"

She drove to the emergency room of the local hospital, where her husband, Mark, works as an administrator. There they gave me eyedrops for inflammation and pain. It took two days resting in a dark room before I recovered enough to go out.

This episode frightened me. Whatever the cause, I began to consider the possibility that I was going to lose my sight. In the middle of my daughter's wedding, I couldn't hide it from the family. It upset me to be the cause of the worry in their voices during a time set aside for celebration.

One episode began in a middle school in Baltimore

where I was managing a consulting project. I had the eyedrops with me so I was able to get through it without an emergency room visit. But my spirits faltered. My work has always been important to me and the position I had at the time was responsible and demanding. It paid far more than a superintendent's salary. By any measure, I had worked hard and proven myself only to have my body betray me.

The worst attack came at the end of a near-perfect vacation with Leonard to France. We had traveled quite a bit by then and always enjoyed it, but this trip set a high-water mark. We flew first class, spent a night in Paris, and then travelled on a refurbished luxury barge through Champagne country. The weather was perfect. We toured important sites in French history, and one morning flew in a hot air balloon that landed in a corn field exactly where a checkered table awaited us with a Champagne breakfast, served by smart-looking young waiters in crisp black-and-white uniforms.

That was only about half of it and the rest was just as magical and exciting and unforgettable!

On the morning of our return home I woke up and opened the blinds. The sudden light stabbed my eyes. I cried out in pain and frustration. "Lord, not NOW!"

I was helpless, but at least we were already headed home. That was another blessing. Leonard got us packed while I sat in a chair with a towel draped over my head to shield my eyes. Wearing a large hat and dark glasses to block the light, I was helpless as Leonard—while trying to manage the luggage alone—guided me out of the hotel, into a cab, into the airport, through security, and finally onto the plane.

Throughout the ordeal Leonard remained quiet, somber, and comforting. "Don't worry, it's going to be all right. We're going to figure out what's going on." But panic was gathering in his voice.

Sleep was impossible, even with a blanket over my head. The episodes always began with pain in the eye and progressed to a terrible headache. In my disorientation and despair, I bargained with the Lord.

"God, whatever this is, just please don't let me die. Please don't let this be permanent. *Please* give somebody the wisdom to figure out what is going on with me because, Lord, I can't live like this."

We finally landed and the crew got us off the airplane as soon as the door opened. Leonard retrieved the car and drove us to the emergency room at Johns Hopkins Hospital's Wilmer Eye Institute, which had been recommended to me earlier. There I was diagnosed as having chronic uveitis, a form of eye inflammation. When I was asked about any other issues, I mentioned my balance and the discarded MS diagnosis.

Around the same time I noticed I was more forgetful than usual. At first I brushed it off as a byproduct of being over-scheduled. I was in the middle of a large, complex, and demanding project in Baltimore to turn around a school from the ground up. My tasks included working with the community to garner support for the initiatives that needed to happen. It was like starting from scratch—rebuilding a failing middle school instructional program, hiring staff, and renovating a building that needed a major overhaul. There were all kinds of emergencies large and small every day. The commute from home was an hour or more each way.

I'm stressed, I told myself. Maybe I'm not getting enough rest because I'm such a night owl and have trouble going to bed at a reasonable hour. When other members of my family noticed my forgetfulness, they said the same thing. "That's Elfreda. Such a workaholic. She's just overdone it."

My sister Debby, a former nurse, was the first of my relatives to have a hunch there was more to it, and her past hunches had usually been right.

One day I was driving home on one of the major highways outside Baltimore when I suddenly realized I didn't recognize where I was. I thought I was getting off the usual exit but then I was driving on streets that were unfamiliar.

"Where the heck am I?" I was driving and driving, talking aloud to myself, seeing no recognizable landmarks, and getting anxious.

"Well, I know I'm not far from home, but I don't know where I am. How can I not know where I am? I'm only twenty minutes from the house." I burst into tears, pulled over, and called my sister Mary at her work.

"Mary!" I blubbered.

"Elfreda, what's the matter? What's the matter?"

"I'm lost!" It was an experience that would terrify anyone, but for someone like myself who is used to being in charge and in command, it was a devastating moment. Suddenly nothing made sense, like in a dream when the harder you try to get somewhere the farther away it seems.

"What do you mean you're lost?"

"I'm lost."

"Are you walking? What do you mean?"

"I'm driving."

"Well, what do you mean?" She was frantic.

"I was on my way home and now I can't figure out how to get there."

She kept saying, "I don't understand. I don't understand. How can you be lost?"

Finally she said, "Okay, where are you? Just stop. Stay where you are. I'll come and get you."

"But I don't know where I am."

"What do you mean?"

"I really don't know where I am. I'm ... just lost." I sobbed.

"Well, what do you see around you?"

"I see a park."

"Okay, Elfreda. We've got to figure out where you are. Maybe we should call 911."

"No, no, no, no, no." I wasn't sick, I told myself. Just lost.

"Oh! The GPS on the phone. I'm just going to type in home and follow the directions."

"Elfreda, wait a minute."

"Never mind. There it is. Never mind. Okay, I've got it. I figured this out. I'll talk to you later"

The GPS got me home and Mary showed up shortly after, bursting through the door. "What was that all about?"

"Oh, that was nothing. I don't know what happened. I must have been so preoccupied I wasn't paying attention and just got lost."

Denial was my friend. The less attention paid to my health the better. I was too busy and professionally satisfied to take time for another layer of doctors and tests to probe this latest symptom. Mary let the issue drop. Wanting to spare Leonard from unnecessary worry, I kept the incident to myself.

The next time it happened I was on a train to New York, but when I got off I found myself in Hartford, Connecticut, and couldn't remember why I was supposed to be there. I stood on the platform muttering to myself, "Okay, pull it together. Don't panic. Where am I?"

I rummaged in my purse for clues and found my ticket to New York. I went into the station and asked the clerk behind the window if the train had passed New York or if it was the next stop.

"That train passed New York two and a half hours ago."

This time I felt no panic. I had just gotten off at the wrong stop and had to buy a ticket back to New York, which I did. I attended to my business in the city and no one knew what had happened.

Another time on the train I was talking to Mary on my cell phone and she asked me where I was.

"I don't know. I think I passed Philadelphia recently. I think I fell asleep, because I'm not sure."

"Elfreda!" She scolded, "That's not safe. You've been falling asleep on the train a lot lately. You could get your briefcase stolen."

The most bizarre and disorienting episode happened at Penn Station in New York on another business trip. When I first got off the train I didn't know where I was. I came out of the station and started looking for signs until I was able to figure it out.

For some reason, I went back inside and sat in the waiting area with my luggage. Then I was hungry and went to one of the sandwich shops and ordered soup and a sandwich. As I ate I had a disturbing thought. *What did I come here for?*

It was a surreal moment. I seemed to feel just fine. I wasn't dizzy, or hallucinating. In fact, my head felt clear. But I had to puzzle out what I was supposed to be doing and where.

Okay. Okay. What do I have to do next? Oh, I have a meeting! And my meeting, I think, starts at one. Better get out of here and get a taxi.

I went up the escalator, out to the curb, and hopped

into a cab. I gave the driver the address and he began to pull away from the curb.

"WAIT! I'm missing something. I don't have my purse. I have to get out! You've got to stop. I had a purse and now I don't. I don't have any money. I have to get out!"

I raced back into the station.

Where was I? Where was I? Where was I? I recognized the waiting room seat where I'd been resting. Oh, no. Where did I go? Oh, I got something to eat!

I found the sandwich shop and the woman at the register spotted me.

"Miss, I was wondering when you were coming back. You know you left your stuff here." She handed me my purse. Thank God!

I turned to go back out to the taxi stand.

"Excuse me," the woman said. "You left your luggage."

Luggage? Why did I need luggage? I'm going to a meeting.

Reunited with luggage and purse, I got into another cab. It took some shuffling through paperwork to find a printout of my hotel reservation.

"Just take me to the Radisson."

Once I was checked in, I called the office to tell them I wasn't feeling well and would be late. I was exhausted from the mental effort of just getting to that point.

I napped, got myself together, went to my meeting, and stayed two nights in the city. I realize I could go spacey any minute and began to second-guess everything I said and did. My eyes also acted up a little one morning, usually the worst time. I dressed in the dark, fumbling with buttons I couldn't see. I managed to get myself home in one piece after two horrible days.

I casually mentioned to Mary that I almost lost my purse and deluded myself into believing I just had a little forgetful spell, which is how I described it to her. But my confidence and sense of security were shaken.

Concealing my problems seemed to be working, mostly. There were moments during meetings or conference calls when I just didn't understand what other people were saying. Then there were some incidents that left me blazing with embarrassment. I was contributing some comments during a meeting when one of the other participants said, "What did you just say? I don't even know what that meant." A long silence followed. Another time I was talking and someone interrupted me to say, "Elfreda, that's not what we're talking about."

Around this time I went to Detroit for the company and on my way to the hotel realized I had misplaced my luggage with my clothes and computer in it. When I got to the hotel I called the Detroit airport security office. My bag had apparently been left unattended somewhere long enough for someone to risk going through it. My laptop and clothes were gone.

Finally, I had an episode that brought it home. Not long after my Detroit trip, I was fixing dinner, had set the table, and wanted some fresh bread to go with it. I called out to Leonard as I went out the door, "I'm going to go to Safeway. I'll be back in ten minutes." The store was a mile from the house.

About a half hour later I was driving when my cell phone rang. It was Leonard. There was a hard edge in his voice.

"Elfreda, I thought you were going to the store? Where are you?"

"That's funny. I'm glad you called. I don't know where I am. I was just driving around." This time I wasn't afraid. In fact, I felt rather content just driving around.

"Elfreda, WHERE—ARE—YOU?"

"I honestly don't know."

The edge was gone, replaced by fear.

"What do you mean you don't know?"

"I just don't know. I don't know where I am."

"Elfreda, can you just pull over and stop?"

"I'm fine, Leonard. There's nothing wrong with me."

"Listen to me! Can you just pull over to a safe spot and park your car?"

"Yeah. I can stop right here. I'm stopped, okay?"

"Okay. Now, tell me the street name. Are you at an intersection?"

"Yes."

"Tell me what the sign says." I told him.

"Stay right there. Just PLEASE stay there. Turn the car off. Don't move. Don't get out of the car. Just wait for me. I'm coming to get you."

I don't remember what happened when he showed up or what happened with my car or what we did or if somebody came with him. I just remember that he came and got me. I don't even remember if we talked about what had happened but that night Leonard was up late in his office, praying.

The next morning Mary called to invite us to her house for dinner, not an unusual invitation under normal circumstances. When we arrived I noticed another car in the driveway and several parked in front of the house. She hadn't mentioned other guests.

Waiting to greet me when I walked in the door were our daughters, both of my sisters, my brother, and a nephew. Nicole was living in North Carolina so I was surprised but happy to see her. I suspected something special was going to happen but it wasn't near a birthday or an anniversary.

After a pleasant dinner, after the table had been cleared, the look on everyone's faces turned sober as they exchanged knowing glances. Mary's eyes began to well.

"Elfreda, we all wanted to talk to you. We're really worried. Something's going on with you. Something serious is happening."

"What do you mean?"

They started telling me all the times they had noticed my forgetfulness. It sounded bad and worse as the stories piled up. Leonard remembered that I was making my favorite German chocolate cake from scratch one day and called him in a tearful panic because I'd made that cake so many times I knew it by heart but suddenly I couldn't remember all the ingredients. Another time I turned one of the stove burners on to cook dinner and completely forgot until Leonard came home and smelled smoke.

Now Mary was telling me, "It's not okay that you're traveling. You can't do that and be safe. You have to stop working until we figure out what's wrong."

"What do you mean? I'm not giving up my job." My work is integral to who I am and at the time it was a dominant factor in how I defined myself.

"You go to New York," she reminded me, "and you leave your purse in a restaurant. You don't know why you're there. You go to the supermarket and you get lost and don't remember why you are where you are, which you don't recognize. Your eyesight has gotten worse. You're having trouble walking. What are we supposed to think?"

Some of it I didn't recall but the experience of having it all laid out like that, with copious tears, was the moment my house of self-delusion came crashing down. They were right. I agreed to see my doctor and tell him all that I had been keeping to myself.

He was stunned. "Here I'm thinking you have this

isolated issue. Now I can tell you this is serious and we need to get to the bottom of this right way. It's beyond what I'm able to diagnose or treat so I'm going to send you to either the National Institutes of Health or Johns Hopkins. Let's start with rheumatology (arthritis and joint disorders) or neurology."

It was November, just before the start of the holiday season. Johns Hopkins gave me an appointment but it was a month away.

A few days later I woke up totally confused. I didn't know what to do, not even what one usually does when waking up. When I managed to sort things out, I called Johns Hopkins to see if I could get in sooner than my scheduled appointment.

"I only live about an hour away. If you have a cancellation any time, can you call me, and I'll take any slot?"

"You can call back every day and see."

The next morning I called. "Do you have any cancellations with any neurologists?" At this point I didn't care which.

"Actually, we have one doctor who had a cancellation. But you'd need to get here in an hour."

"I'm on my way!"

Part IV:
The Power of Faith

Fourteen:

But Do You KNOW Him?

I drove myself without incident into Baltimore to see the neurologist. After I recounted all my symptoms he said, "Let's map out a plan. We're going to start from head to toe. Ever had a CAT scan?"

"Nope."

"MRI?"

"Nope. I'm not sure that I even know the difference."

It took several weeks to get on the schedule and the scan was done just before Christmas. Two days after Christmas I woke to the phone ringing. It was morning but barely dawn.

"Mrs. Massie, this is Dr. Probasco."

"Hello, doctor. How are you?"

"Mrs. Massie, we got the results from the scan, and we need you to come in right away. I'm afraid we found something, a sizable mass."

I yawned. "Excuse me. What does that mean?"

"We don't know yet what it means, but we need

you to come in right away so that we can take a look at this. Okay?"

"Okay," I said, and hung up.

I woke Leonard. "That was the doctor's office. They want me to come in. They said they saw something, a mass or something, and they wanted to talk to me about it or do some more tests."

I was having guests for dinner that evening. I didn't have time for this.

"Okay," Leonard said. "When do they want you to come in?"

"He sounded like I should come in today. But I'm tired. I have so much to do for tonight. I'm going back to sleep for a bit."

An hour or so later, the phone rang again.

"Mrs. Massie, this is Dr. Probasco again. Are you on your way?"

"No. I fell back to sleep."

"Listen, we need you to come in now. We have a team waiting for you."

That jolted me awake.

"What do you mean? Is it serious?"

"Yes, it's very serious."

"Well, okay." I must have sounded hesitant.

"Look, if you don't want to come to Hopkins, then you need to go to your nearest emergency room right away. They can call us and we'll talk to them."

"No. That's all right. I'll be there as soon as I can."

Leonard had already lurched into high gear. We dressed, put on our warm coats, and as we walked to the car I said, "I'm hungry. Why don't we stop and eat first. We're probably going to spend all day sitting in an emergency room. At least I won't be starving."

"Don't you think we need to get to the hospital,

Elfreda? Didn't he tell you to come right away?"

"I'm hungry. Let's just go. It won't slow us down all that much."

I look back on it now and think, poor Leonard! He must have been out of his mind with worry as we sat in that restaurant eating a meal while the minutes ticked away. I can't say I wasn't worried, but this was the umpteenth time I'd made such a trip, to see a doctor or to visit an emergency room. I was in no hurry to learn what the doctor was in a such a hurry to see me about.

We were halfway through our lunch when my cell phone rang. I fished it out of my purse, thinking it might be one of the girls calling about holiday plans.

"MRS. MASSIE!" Dr. Probasco's voice was all steel. "This is VERY serious. You really need to get here RIGHT away. We are waiting for you."

"Okay, okay. But about how long do you think this is going to take? I mean, it's Christmas and I have company and ... "

He guffawed. "HA! How long is it going to take? Mrs. Massie, we're admitting you to the hospital today. We have a bed waiting."

Geez. Why didn't he say so the first time?

"Admitted? But I didn't bring an overnight bag."

At that point Leonard had reached the limit of his endless patience.

"All right, Elfreda! Let's go. Get up from the table. Right now!"

He threw down some bills for the check, held out my coat while I put it on, and we drove the distance into Baltimore in trembling silence. We were about to share another medical crisis, only this time we knew it in advance instead of waking up on the side of a mountain road on a winter night.

While I was being admitted, Leonard drove to the offices of my other doctors to gather all my records. I might need a biopsy, they said. Finally, on the morning of New Year's Eve—after days of tests, fear, boredom, and prayer—a nurse told me I would be discharged later that day.

"That's wonderful," I said. "Now I can go the church tonight." Every New Year's Eve our tradition is to go to church, sing, and talk about the blessings of the year, how great the year was, or how bad it was, and how great the next one will be. It's a less formal service than Sunday morning worship, followed by a community meal.

The nurse said she didn't think I would be going anywhere except home to bed, but I felt okay and changed into my street clothes. Leonard was there, so I figured we'd just sit and wait until I could officially be discharged.

A hour or so later, a gaggle of doctors in white jackets crowded into my hospital room, led by Dr. Michael Lim, a leading brain tumor specialist at Hopkins. The others were his students. Dr. Lim introduced himself and then said, "You know, I wasn't necessarily discharging you." He had a sober demeanor, all business.

My heart sank. "I want to go home."

"Okay, you can go home. But you have to do some follow-up with us."

He explained that they found a tumor and it needed to be biopsied. He described it as massive, covering the left quadrant of my head. It was an unusual kind of brain tumor, a bony mass that was taking over the left quadrant of my face—lymphangioma of the skull base. All my symptoms were a result of pressure that this mass was putting on brain tissue and nerves.

My next consultation would be with a surgeon who

would have to do an unusual kind of biopsy, going into the area under the skull—through my nose. A little dazed and overwhelmed, I started to cry. All these doctors and now they want to bring in another?

Finally Dr. Lim and his ducklings left and Leonard took me out to the car.

When he got in and closed his door, I said, "I don't want to go home yet. I just want to go to church." I needed to be in the fellowship of people I knew. I needed to be with music.

Two weeks later they did the biopsy, which I thought would be a minor procedure. It was a hideous experience. They had to create an opening in my sinuses so they could insert these tiny tools through my nose and into the space under my brain. The growth was in the back of my head, near the spinal column, so it was a long surgery using a tiny camera that had to snake its way around to get to it.

When I was recovered enough to look into a mirror my face was distorted from swelling and unrecognizable—eyes shut, nose swollen and packed with cotton. The new specialist who had done the biopsy, Dr. Kofi Boahene, said he would be in touch in about a week to report the findings.

Before leaving his office, I told him, "Dr. Boahene, here's the deal. If you find out what this is, and if for any reason at all you have some really bad news, do not tell me in front of my family. Do not call me in to your office with Leonard and my daughters to deliver it. I want you to call and talk to me privately, so I can process what you have to say."

He agreed and sent me home with a large ice pack over my face. For the next two weeks I had the worst headache in the world.

I had been told that Dr. Boahene was the best surgeon

in the world for the procedure I needed to have. I had no way to judge that. He was charismatic and exotic—deep brown skin, distinctly round head, brilliant smile, and a pronounced accent. I had to ask him a couple of times to repeat what he was saying, on top of my ears and mind struggling to process it.

I didn't know much about Dr. Boahene in the beginning but I came to learn he is an extraordinary surgeon with a remarkable personal story. He was the firstborn of eight children of a bookseller (his father) and a bank teller (his mother) in Ghana. His father had switched careers and became a drug company representative and then opened a chemist shop dispensing common remedies for common ailments like malaria and dysentery.

When a coup upended the economy and the politics of Ghana, his family lost virtually everything. His parents, active in the worldwide Christian missionary movement, struggled to make ends meet.

Dr. Boahene had decided as a child that he wanted to be a doctor. As the firstborn and a boy, he grew up with a keen sense of responsibility for his family's future, which would eventually include seven brothers and sisters. He had met and exceeded all expectations.

He made perfect marks in high school and then, by a circuitous and international route, got himself to the States. He earned his medical degree from Meharry Medical College, one of two historically black medical schools with long storied pasts.

When I met him he was a recognized expert in his specialty and active as a surgical missionary, flying with teams and equipment to Africa and other underserved parts of the world. He performed repair surgeries on children with cleft lips and palates; disfigurements from trauma, birth defect, or disease; and facial nerve damage.

Waiting for his call made that the longest seven days I can remember. And then ... no call. The month ended. Super Bowl Sunday came and went.

The call finally came one Sunday morning, right after Leonard left for church. I wasn't feeling well and decided to stay home. At first I was startled to hear his voice. It was an unusual day for a doctor to be calling, an unusual time, and I didn't know what to make of the fact that he was making the call himself and not an assistant. Then I remembered my instructions to him to tell me alone if it was bad news. I grabbed a discarded envelope from the trash, found a pencil, and braced myself.

"I don't have good news," he began. "We're not absolutely sure what it is, but we do know it's quite rare. We need to try to remove as much of this as we can."

With trembling hand I scribbled as best I could. With the adrenaline rush I'd forget all but a detail here and there to tell Leonard. It took a minute or so until I actually grasped what he was proposing.

Something in my skull.

Malicious.

Bones.

Nasty bone replaces good bone.

Surgery. Soon.

This can't be true, I thought. I read my notes over and over again. I thought about calling Dr. Boahene back to ask him to repeat the message.

Instead I just sat there, still and quiet on the edge of the bed, for about a half hour. The music had suddenly changed. Now so would the dance. I had never felt so vulnerable.

I cry infrequently and when I do it's usually about happy things or music that moves my soul. I also cry when I'm terrified. When I heard the rumble of the garage door—Leonard returning from church and parking the car—I took up position by the door. When it opened I burst into tears.

After choking out the news between sobs, I said, "How are they going to do something like that with my brain? I don't want anybody going in my head. I don't want my skull cracked!" The thought of it was just too creepy.

A few days later Leonard and I were sitting in Dr. Boahene's office at Johns Hopkins watching him hold a human skull in one hand and motioning with a pencil in the other. I had just told him, "I don't want the whole side of my face removed and I don't want plastic surgery."

Poking his pencil through openings in the skull, Dr. Boahene explained how he could avoid opening my skull to get to the mass. "Like this, we can push the eyeball just a tiny bit out of the way and go like this, and like this with miniaturized instruments and a camera. It's somewhat an experimental procedure, still somewhat radical. But I've done it before."

While a brain surgeon "compressed" my brain so it would be out of harm's way, Dr. Boahene was going to go through my eye socket and under my brain to the site of the mass. Then he would chip away enough of the nasty bony stuff so there would be extra space in case it continued to grow.

My symptoms were severe enough that doing nothing was not an option. I could endanger myself or other people the way things were going. The doctor's demeanor, his credentials, and his attention to detail were all impeccable. Johns Hopkins has an unassailable reputation.

However, I said, "You've only done this surgery a few times, right?"

"Yes. Very successfully."

"And you want to try it on me? You want to go in through my eyelid and start removing a tumor."

After some further explanation, I asked him, "If I were your mother and your mother had this, what would you recommend to me?"

He smiled confidently. "If you were my mother, I would do just as we have done—do the biopsy and based on those results, I'd suggest we take out as much as we can."

I pondered that for a moment. Maybe his mother wasn't the best test. Maybe she was elderly and the gain might not be worth the pain.

"Okay. Now, what if I were your younger sister?"

"I would recommend the same thing."

All that was well and good but I considered the possibility that it might take a miracle—a little help from the Lord. I wanted to be sure whoever was going to be poking around in my brain was someone who was not apathetic or callous about the surgery or about me. I needed to feel some spiritual alignment—a surgeon who stood with me spiritually, who believed as much as I did that God was going to bring me through this, who I believed God was speaking to. That had been my prayer all along. God, please send me to the right people and please guide them and provide them with wisdom and knowledge.

After we had discussed the surgery and it felt like time to wrap up and go home, that's when I asked him the big question: "Do you believe in God?" and he replied, "The real question is, Do you *know* Him?"

That was it! He was the one. It's something to believe in Him. But to know Him means to walk with Him, talk with Him, be on intimate terms with Him.

"We're good," I said. "Now I'm going to be praying about this. I'm going to pray for you. I'm going to pray that God guides your hands."

"So will I."

Fifteen:

In The Arms of Jesus

Nicole was about to be ordained as a minister in Charlotte, North Carolina. It was a major life and family event and nothing could keep me away, not even an urgent major surgery. Around the same time, our church was holding a special service and gathering to celebrate the anniversary of Leonard becoming the pastor.

After the date for surgery was set and I had acknowledged all the risks by signing the permission forms—blindness, loss of sense of smell and taste, paralysis, death—I had to consider the possibility I might not make it. I used the extra time I had to prepare. I attempted to enlist Leonard to help assemble all my insurance documents and get my affairs in order, but he found it too upsetting. What conversations we had about "it" were cryptic.

He'd ask, "You okay?"

"I'm good. God's got this. Are you okay?"

"Yeah, I'm okay."

But his eyes would brim with tears and he'd take my hand and wordlessly squeeze it. Just about everyone in my family and among my friends squirmed when I raised the possibility of my dying. My daughter Michelle, who lived nearby, agreed to help get my paperwork in order.

Taking stock of my life under those circumstances helped me focus on the big stuff. There was so much to be grateful for. I had known love fully. I had beloved, treasured friends. We had smart healthy daughters. I'd given of myself to others. I'd talked to God and turned my life over to Him. What I might have regretted was trivial by comparison and easy to dismiss.

After Nicole's ordination and the celebration for Leonard, the dreaded day arrived. Once I was checked in to the hospital and being prepped, Dr. Boahene came to see me. I had asked for a final private conversation. As he went over the procedure again I had to fight a wave of terror and brush away a few tears.

Doing my best to sound brave and ready, I asked, "So, Dr. Boahene, you feeling good?"

"I'm good," he said confidently.

"You feeling sure? You feeling really good, sure-footed?"

"I'm good. I'm ready. And what about you? Are you ready?"

"I'm ... sort of ready."

After he left I had a last pre-op conversation with God.

Well, Lord, if this is it, my life is in Your hands. If it's my time to go, then please take me peacefully and spare my family any unnecessary suffering.

Then I was wheeled on a gurney to a waiting area where my family and friends could be with me just before

I went into the operating room. It was quite a crowd. I did nothing to discourage people from coming as I wanted to see everybody I cared about one more time—in case I died. The occasion seemed to need a unifying message so I called out to get everyone's attention.

"Excuse me, folks. Listen, I'm going to tell everybody right now—if I don't come out, you'll see me on the other side."

I scanned the mob of long faces with glistening eyes. The love I felt gave me courage and solace. I thought, *How blessed I am!*

"If you believe in God, and you believe there's an afterlife, that we're all going to be together in Heaven, just know I'll be waiting there for you. You'll see me."

Moments later the anesthesiologist arrived to help wheel me into the operating room.

"Hey!" I said cheerily. "I want to know about you. Do you believe in God?"

"Absolutely, ma'am."

"Well, I AM in good hands. I have two God-fearing men by my side. I'm feeling good now. I'm ready. Let's do this."

Once I was in the operating room, the anesthesiologist looked down at me and said, "Think some pleasant thoughts."

The big lamp overhead was like a giant sun so I closed my eyes and imagined myself on a beach. I started singing and the last thing I remember is the anesthesiologist's voice saying, "Okay. She's out."

Sometime between the surgery and when I woke up in the intensive care unit I dreamed that Jesus was holding me in His arms and rocking me like a baby. I wondered where He was taking me. I felt as light as air, content and utterly peaceful.

The first time I woke up, Dr. Boahene's gentle voice was in my ear. I couldn't see much, what with the bandages and swelling. Everything had gone well, he said. It had been a seven-hour surgery and they had removed about half of the mass.

The next time I remember waking, Leonard was by my side. Then my mother, Debby, and Mary. They said I had been whispering in my sleep, over and over, "I'm in the arms of Jesus. I'm in the arms of Jesus."

They had wept with joy. "She's fine! She's in the arms of Jesus."

Sixteen:

Just Me And The Abyss

The surgery was a medical success. Dr. Boahene was able to remove enough of the affected bone to make a big difference in the quality of my life, although the recovery was gradual and would never be complete.

I went home from the hospital looking and feeling even worse than I had after the through-the-sinus biopsy three months earlier. My face was newly swollen, I couldn't see out of my left eye, and I was emotionally and physically depleted. I was a proud prize fighter faced with the possibility that I'd just fought my last round. I began to feel hollowed out.

It was April 2011. It had been five years since the second knee surgery. That had been followed by the RSD in my leg, gallbladder removal, hysterectomy to remove a nine-pound tumor, pericarditis (inflammation around the heart), pleurisy that bloomed into pneumonia, tumorous growths in my throat, a lumpectomy, and I had been misdiagnosed at one time or another with iritis, multiple sclerosis, lupus, rheumatoid arthritis, and a few other maladies I can't remember.

During my recovery I joked with friends and family that "There's no other part of my body left to fix." There was, however, my psyche. That would take much more time to heal than my face, and no amount of surgery could help. The psychic pain came from the blow that all this had delivered to my self-confidence and sense of empowerment, and from the anxiety about the effect my health would have on my professional life.

Before the surgery I had arranged with the consulting company I worked for to reduce my travel and responsibilities until I was up to it again. I was being paid a monthly retainer for which I was communicating with superintendents from around the country, arranging calls and visits, and helping with sales strategy. Once I got better, I hoped to do more and get back on top of my game.

We had become used to a healthy income and on the basis of my bright future we'd moved into a new home that, like millions of other families, we purchased with an unfavorable mortgage near a peak in the real estate market.

The folks who owned the consulting company had been encouraging. "We'd like to keep you on. We really want you to help us by doing some consulting."

Shortly after the time of my operation, the firm hired a new CEO. A former coworker told me my name had come up in a management conversation. "This Dr. Massie. She's on medical leave, right? So, tell me again why we're still paying her? Someone who's basically brain-dead?"

That was hard to hear at the time. I was still recovering and it sounded like the new regime had written me off as dead weight, to be heaved overboard so the ship would go faster. It was so careless and cruel. Looking back, there must have been rumors in the company about my memory gaps and uneven performance in meetings. Add brain surgery and it's not hard to imagine people who didn't know me assuming I was a lost cause.

Then I got an email from the company announcing that they were reorganizing and forming a high-level advisory board. Would I be willing to stay as a member of the advisory board on a retainer?

That sounded like a good option. They asked for an updated version of my résumé. I thought, *What's changed since I started with the company—other than the surgery? Is this some sort of joke?*

I sent the résumé. Several days passed with no follow-up messages or calls. May ended without any communication about the reorganization. I hoped it was just a glitch.

Then I heard that some full-time employees had been let go and my colleagues shared a rumor that I was next. June's check came, but May's never showed up. My spirits sank.

Finally, near the end of July, I got a call from an executive I had worked with, someone I had trusted and with whom I felt a measure of professional camaraderie. His voice was tight.

"Elfreda, how ... how are you? Wow, what a lot you've been dealing with, right? Wow. But I guess you're doing okay, now. Right? Anyway... Listen, um, Elfreda... um, there's something I want to talk to you about."

I allowed myself an audible sigh. "Okay. What is it?"

"Well, listen, unfortunately we've had to let some people go. Well ... heh ... you probably heard about all that. Yeah, so ... Um, so... I guess we just don't quite know how ... um ... well, if... if we're going to be able to keep you."

I had no patience for verbal footsie.

"Look, are you saying you don't know IF you'll be able to keep me, or are you calling to tell me that you're letting me go?"

"Well, Elfreda … um … I'm so glad you understand. Yeah. We're, you see, in sort of a spot and … well… So, listen .. uh … can you just get something to me today? Like before the end of the day. Just an email saying you're … um … resigning. I need to have it before the first of August."

I shook my head in silent disgust.

"You know, this isn't quite what I expected to hear from you. What I'm willing to put in writing is documentation that you called me today. I'm willing to do that."

"Okay, great … um … that should be … um … that's fine, I guess. Just so I have it before the end of the month. Of course we'll pay you for August. That's the least … well, you know."

Those were the last words I ever heard from that fellow. The following week I sent an email to the new CEO, copied to my attorney. That got the response I was looking for: "Your check is in the mail." And it was.

Now what? There would be no more working for people who lacked the grace and presence of mind to call me and say, "Elfreda, money's tight and the new guy— we all know you—he doesn't understand your value."

Word of my separation spread through the educational consulting community, generating offers from other companies that did understand my value. "Would you like to come and help us? When you're ready, just call. We'll even create a job for you."

It was flattering and reassuring to know I had a good reputation and something to contribute. Thinking about what I'd been through and was still recovering from, I worried about joining a new corporate team and then having to explain things like, "I couldn't follow through today because I had a medical appointment and couldn't change it."

My heart of hearts wanted to chirp, "Yes! Of course I'll do it!" That had been the North Star of my life. Being needed fills my soul. Instead I was a little coy, leaving the door ajar. "Okay. If you come up with something for me we can talk about it then."

Now it was just me and the abyss. My body had been betraying me for five years. It occurred to me that I might be stuck in a spiral. Were my best days behind me? Had I already spent the last day I would ever feel healthy?

Being knocked off the summit of my career was even more crushing. My work and my ethos—helping children become healthy, productive adults—had dominated how I defined myself for four decades. I was like a pianist who'd lost her hands or a painter who'd lost her vision. I'd become a shell of the Elfreda Massie I had once been. I looked about the same, but it was a vessel that had been emptied. How was I going to fill it back up? I prayed, I read, and I pondered.

One day I was visiting with my sister Mary, and we were speculating about the future when an idea popped into my head that gave me the first real jolt of excitement I'd felt in a long time.

"You know how everybody in the family relies on me to help them plan their trips and vacations? Remember back in Pittsburgh how I was all set to go be a stewardess and see the world before I started teaching? I think I'd like to try being a travel agent now."

"That's right!" she said. "And you've already traveled so much and been a lot of places. You're always making recommendations for places to go."

I knew a lot about travel as a consumer, but not much about the industry. I did some research and decided to buy a travel franchise. Mary agreed to partner with me and split the investment cost. I used my contacts and powers of persuasion, and soon I was in business. I was a micro-agency, but I began to travel again, this time with more confidence than I'd had in a while. No more debilitating iritis and all the other things that had made travel worrisome. It's what I do today and I love it. But getting here took a lot of hard work and faith.

At first the brain surgery seemed to have robbed me of all the things that defined me. Owning a travel agency was great but it wasn't why I earned my doctorate. In time I began to see that I'm much more than my professional competency in education. There were aspects of my personality that I had never explored and wouldn't have unless I first lost the Elfreda I thought I was. I still mourn her at times and would love to be her again.

I've had to accept that there are things I'm just not going to be able to do, or not in the same way. I try to always remember that while everybody else is at the education conferences hanging out and changing the world, I'm doing something that's more fun and less stressful.

While I'm not doing quite what I used to do, I can create each day to be whatever I want. And, as I write this, I have been consulting again, for the National Center on Education and the Economy in Washington. The NCEE is a nonprofit education think tank originally started by the Carnegie Corporation to study and encourage reform in the American school system. NCEE's mission is to research and benchmark the world's highest performing school systems. My role is to help train school principals and district leaders in leadership strategy, subject area knowledge, and best practices to improve teaching and learning.

For another Washington-based nonprofit, EdFuel, I serve as an executive coach. EdFuel provides leadership development and individual coaching to the education community. Out of all this I've come to believe that our connectedness with each other and ourselves is based more on our pain and disappointments than on our accomplishments and successes. We all at some point in our lives experience a biological or psychological crisis or slump. What matters is how we deal with it, avoiding getting bogged down in the negative stuff.

I have found that the way to get through a crisis or a challenge is threefold: reimagining, as I did when I was determined to walk again; rethinking, as I have done throughout my career in education; and re-creating, as I have done by changing careers. It's taken me a lifetime to connect those dots, but I realize now that it's also the message I got as a child, although in a less structured way.

Perhaps this is a thought process that's unique to African Americans. In the past, when black people encountered obstacles they had few options. The choice was to adapt and reimagine themselves, or turn those negative emotions inward, which is one reason for the high rate of dysfunction among black families. This is a process I believe all people could use.

My decision to stay near home and go to college at Pitt instead of being a racial pioneer at Sarah Lawrence was a process of reimagining myself. Instead of being a groundbreaker I ended up following in the footsteps of my relatives who were teachers and program administrators. I'm just as proud of that as I would have been had I attended Sarah Lawrence and achieved success in some other way.

A scripture lesson that's widely taught in Baptist churches begins with the question, "Whose report are you going to believe?" The lesson teaches us to believe the report of the Lord as opposed to the report of mere humans.

A doctor may report to you that you have cancer and the prognosis for survival is poor. However, the report we should believe is the Lord's, which gives us hope, which in turn gives us comfort. When people are comforted and hopeful, they are more likely to get better. That's how faith heals. In the end, the doctor is guessing, however expertly. Only God knows. His is the report we should believe.

As a result of all my experiences, I've had a few insights about dealing with grief, pain, and disappointment—yours as well as those of people you love.

- Lean on a trusted friend. That should be someone you trust to listen when you just need to vent, without offering advice and solutions.

  Responding to a hurting person with solutions puts the burden on them to act. If they don't, or they disagree with the suggestions, a helpful friend is likely to say, "Well, I told you what to do. Why didn't you just do it?"

  A dependency can develop by relying on problems solvers. The hurting person shifts responsibility to the helper to figure everything out. And if the solution doesn't pan out, they may think, "Well, I did what she told me to do, but it didn't work. I can't trust her."

  Sometimes you've just got to tell someone, "I feel awful today." My friend, Joan, was diagnosed with pancreatic cancer about the same time I was diagnosed with my brain tumor. We spoke when I was in the hospital.

  "Can you believe this?" she said. "Can you believe they said I have pancreatic cancer?"

And I said, "Yes, I know how you feel. I can't believe they told me I have a brain tumor."
We'd talk like that every so often and we both said, "Yes, I know," over and over again.

- Don't give in, give out. One way to turn around a bad day is to find someone who is having a worse day and do something nice for them. My friend with pancreatic cancer actually cooked my favorite foods and had her daughter deliver them to me. I've done similar things myself many times, sending a fruit basket, a cookie bouquet, or a floral arrangement. Sometimes it's a visit, or even just a call. Cheering up someone else will cheer you up too.

- Dump the downers. A crisis can be when you've got to let some people exit your life. I've had to do that with some so-called friends who were naysayers and seemed to think my future was doom and gloom and let me know about it. The last thing I wanted to hear was someone telling me their stories of pain and despair. Cut those people loose and gather up some friends with positive energy to share.

- Talk to God. There were times during my medical calamities that I felt I was going through them alone. During those times I just talked to God. I prayed that He would heal my body. My supplications would go something like, "God, you know this body. You made me. You know what's going on, and I trust that you're going to reveal it to me or to one of these doctors and we're going to get on with it.

"I'm going to hang in here and I'm not going

to give up, Lord. I know I'm not supposed to understand everything, but you can see I'm wearing thin. I don't know how much longer I can take this." I couldn't see it at the time, but He was listening and working it out in my favor. I weathered the storm.

- God leads doctors, not the other way around. Having faith means you understand that doctors can do some amazing things in the operating room but healing comes from God and from within yourself. That's why when I'm discussing my health with a new doctor, I interview him or her. As a result, most of my doctors at some point have become my friends. Sometimes one of them will call to check on me, or say, "You know, I just ran across your name or somebody mentioned you and I thought I'd call and find out how you are doing."

  I do the same, sometimes sending a doctor a note to say, "Just thinking about you. Thanks again for your care. You're the greatest."

- Why me? I began drafting thoughts for this book after my brain tumor was removed and one of the entries began with "Why me?" It's a question without an answer. It suggests that you were chosen to suffer instead of someone else, which isn't the way God works in our lives. "Why me?" suggests you are being victimized instead of having your faith tested or some other divine design that you can't possibly know about.

  When I shared this conversation with Nicole, her response was perfect. "I don't know, Mom. Why *not* you?"

———

With all the knowledge and insights I've gained, I'm still trying to figure out who I am and what I do. I knew who I was before. Now I'm not sure. I'm still trying to figure out my purpose. Before, when asked, "What do you do?" I was clear. I'm an educator, a music director at my church, a devoted daughter, spouse, and mother.

Now it's a stumble—"Well, I used to..." or, "I'm sort of retired." I don't know why, but it's hard for me to say, "I had to stop working because I had a health issue."

My mother once told me, "The word retirement is not in the Bible, so there's always work to do." That struck a chord with me and my experiences repeatedly confirm how true it is.

Epilogue:
Welcome Home!

I f you are white and happen to visit a historic
site known as the Elkridge Furnace Inn, located
between Baltimore and Washington, you will find a
beautifully preserved plantation-style brick mansion
surrounded by lush, tidy gardens. There's an elegant
dining room inside, and after your meal you can
wander the grounds and learn a bit about the history
of American iron-making from the eighteenth and
early nineteenth centuries. The brochure will inform
you about the noted owners of Elkridge and their
golden pasts of plenty and privilege. It's a world you
could fantasize living in.

If you are black, as you get out of your car in the
parking lot the first thought that may come to mind
is, "Where did our people sleep? Where are the slave
quarters?" They are behind the main house at Elkridge,
a couple of claptrap wooden huts, likely reproductions,

which one white visitor wrote about on a travel blog as "kind of gimmicky to have around as a point of interest." Such is the often invisible history of African Americans.

Leonard and I went to Elkridge once for dinner. It's a beautiful place and we both wondered how many slaves it must have taken to keep it up. As we walked into the mansion we couldn't picture ourselves in that part of its history, even less so having dinner. How amazed the slaves would be if they could see us now, I thought, sitting in a grand, glittering dining room enjoying a gourmet meal served on a linen tablecloth by waiters wearing white gloves.

So much of African American history is like that. Behind the story of many of America's most hallowed institutions and historical sites is a hidden history that many black people are keenly alert to and intensely curious about. Evidence of the growth of that interest is the popularity of a recent remake of the 1977 hit miniseries *Roots*. We are evolving as a culture and realizing that our history is incomplete. There are interruptions and gaps. Our written history is sparse so what we know is based mostly on oral retelling.

I've chosen to end this literary journey about where it began, to emphasize the importance of family narrative in shaping our lives and defining who we are and what our destinies might be. This is an exciting time for African American genealogy and history. Many public records are now available on the Internet. Relentless investigators like Harvard's Henry Louis Gates Jr. have been digging up such treasures as the first books by African American writers and previously unknown family histories of noted African Americans. Thanks to DNA technology, we can even unlock our history all the way back to Africa.

Happily, this awareness and yearning to know and

comprehend is spreading to younger generations. Our daughter Michelle went with her husband once to Charleston, South Carolina, the city where about half of all enslaved Africans first set foot in North America. In terms of hallowed ancestral ground, Charleston's slave market is the closest thing we have to an Ellis Island. They visited a few of the many restored mansions, all built and paid for by slave labor, and came back with similar thoughts to the ones we'd had at Elkridge.

"Mom, do you realize, in all that heat, how grueling it must have been for the slaves working on those plantations? Not being able to change your clothes, and being so sweaty but having to look clean when you're serving food, and working in those outdoor kitchens?"

Visiting a place like the site of Charleston's slave market reminds us of the thing we have in common with most non-Native Americans. Someone in our past—from whom we inherited our blood, our complexions, and our history—suffered some of the most dreadful experiences a human can have, survived, and somehow made a new life in a foreign land. That resilience is what's meant by the African proverb which gives this book its title: "When the music changes, so does the dance."

The power of family and cultural history is hard to over-estimate. Jews, even those without relatives who died in the Holocaust, are invariably moved to tears when they visit places like Auschwitz. It touches that part of them that feels connected to the tragic story of the Jewish people.

African descendants who visit historic slavery sites often feel similar emotions. It's a grief we yearn to experience as part of reconstructing or reaffirming our narratives. That would seem to be one explanation for why a 2014 University of Minnesota study found that two-thirds of African Americans spend their vacations in the slave states of the old South. We want to go backward in time because it gives us courage and meaning for continuing forward. If they could make it, so can we!

Of all Americans living today, about 85 percent were born in the US, all of them except Native Americans with an immigrant story somewhere in their family background. The vast majority of us have mixed histories, able to trace our ancestors back to multiple cultures. That's especially true for African Americans, except that before Barack Obama was elected president it surprised white people when a black person took an interest in his or her white ancestors. It was big news in 2009 when Muhammad Ali, an iconic figure in African American culture, went to Ennis, County Clare, Ireland, where his great-grandfather, Abe Grady, was born. A crowd of 10,000 turned out to welcome Ali as a son of Ireland!

When I was younger and we were all concerned with the upheavals of the times—the civil rights movement, black political power, desegregation—I didn't have a sense of pride about the past. Most of us didn't even understand that there was a history. In the books we read, every famous person with the exception of a few people like George Washington Carver was white.

We've come a long way. Today there are many tours of sites important in the history of slavery, especially the Underground Railroad. Historical dramas on television increasingly feature black characters based on real people. The show *Hell On Wheels*, about the building of the cross-continental railroad, has featured people like Stagecoach Mary (Mary Fields), the first African American mail carrier in America, and, in her time, a respected and revered resident of Cascade, Montana.

A couple of years ago, BBC America produced a show

called *Copper*, about a New York detective in 1864 who relies on a black medical doctor for his forensic investigations. Ato Essandoh, the actor who portrayed the character of Dr. Matthew Freeman, said he was skeptical when he first read the script that such a person could have existed. He thought, "That was impossible."

He told an interviewer, "For an actor, you need to feel grounded in the reality of what you're doing. I looked it up, and there were actually six or seven that existed in New York. That's where I found my anchor, and I found the reality of what I could do."

Until recently, people sort of assumed that life for African Americans started when we were slaves. Now we are following the trail all the way to Africa. I am one of those who did, thanks to the actress Cicely Tyson. In 2007 I participated in a training conference where Dr. Tyson was the keynote speaker. We met and hit it off. Out of that connection came the gift of hearing my daughter Michelle say she knows I'm her mother. Dr. Tyson used our home to film interviews with mothers and daughters from different cultures for a documentary project.

One morning before the first interview of the day, she and I were sitting at the breakfast table and a thought popped into my head. "You know, I have this feeling that I'm going to go to Africa this year."

Her face lit up. "Really? Is that something you want to do?"

"Yes. I really want to go to Africa. I went to Egypt, but that was a long time ago. This time I want to have a more personal experience and find out more about who I am. I want to know more about what Africa is and not just what I read."

A few days later she asked again. "You really want to go to Africa?"

"Definitely, and I just know I'm going to go this year."

"Well," she said, a sparkle in her eye, "do you mind if I pass your name on to Bob Johnson?"

Robert L. Johnson founded Black Entertainment Television (BET) and became the first black billionaire when he sold the company. He and Dr. Tyson had worked on several projects for his foundation.

"For what?"

"He is looking for someone who knows education systems for a fact-finding team Bob is putting together to go to Liberia and see what can be done to help the new government rebuild."

Johnson had created the Liberia Enterprise Development Fund with a $30 million investment to provide credit for Liberian entrepreneurs. In making the announcement, he said he would lead a four-day business and cultural mission to get the ball rolling.

I knew something about Liberia—from the Latin word that means land of the free—because of its role in black history as a clumsy, largely failed experiment promoted by abolitionists and slaveholders alike to "repatriate" (expel) freed slaves from America. With the encouragement of politicians like Presidents Lincoln and Monroe, organizations in several states helped establish colonies for them in the region of West Africa that eventually became Liberia.

An estimated 13,000 freed slaves had settled there by the time the Back To Africa movement died out in the late nineteenth century. The problem was that the freed slaves were so far removed from the cultures of their ancestors that they had no interest in going back or submitting to the rule of the indigenous people.

When I was invited to join Robert Johnson's team in 2007, Liberia was recovering from a bloody civil war that had lasted fourteen years and left many men with hacked-off hands and arms. Now things were looking up. The country had just elected Africa's first woman head of state, President Ellen Johnson Sirleaf. She was popular, in much the same vein as Nelson Mandela was in South Africa—a principled, educated reformer.

Robert Johnson had adopted Liberia because African Americans "have a responsibility to support Liberia, much like Jewish Americans support Israel. We have a special responsibility to do whatever we can to ensure that President Sirleaf succeeds."

I couldn't have been more excited to be going along.

In addition to Dr. Tyson, the team included the late Walter J. Leonard, assistant director of admissions at Harvard who, in the late 1960s, introduced the affirmative action formula that eventually spread across the country, opening doors for so many women and minorities. Also on board were Morris Goldfarb, CEO of G-III, an apparel conglomerate started by his father, a Holocaust survivor; and Rodney Slater, an African American who had been Secretary of Transportation during President Bill Clinton's second term.

My role was to look at the schools and educational system and try to figure out how to rebuild them after fourteen years of destruction and disruption. Our delegation of twenty-five people would also visit businesses in Monrovia (named for US President James Monroe), tour villages in the countryside, and meet with Liberians from all walks of life.

My brother, sister, and daughters had been to Africa and shared their stories about the emotional moment when they first set foot on African soil. My experience fulfilled my expectations and then some. As the private jet we flew on was making its final approach, I could hear—or more accurately feel—the beating of drums. My heart began to hammer in my chest. Was I was having an anxiety attack? Was I so wound up that I was imagining things? When I looked around, others were nodding and saying, "Do you feel that? Do you hear it?"

The source was a massive crowd of Liberians who had come out to the airport to greet our entourage. They were all beating drums, so many and so loudly we could detect the sound from inside the plane. That gave me goose bumps.

Everybody in Liberia knew who Cicely Tyson and Robert Johnson were and they all seemed to be at the airport that day. The country was still celebrating the end of the violence and the beginning of a new era. The air thrummed with excitement as I walked down the short stairway from the plane to the tarmac. The drumming was louder and there was also singing and shouting. The mob of smiling Liberians swarmed over us, hugging us with faces shining with tears of joy, handing us little Liberian flags and other souvenirs.

"Welcome home! Welcome home! Welcome home!"

I looked around and for the first time in my life found myself in a country where everybody looked like me. It did feel as though I was coming home. My heart overflowed and I wept, as did many of my fellow travelers.

That was one of the most profound moments in my life. I'd found a part of my identity I hadn't known was missing until it fit perfectly into place. My family narrative, which until then went back only as far as a cotton field in South Carolina, had in a single bound leaped the Atlantic Ocean and traveled hundreds of years backward in time.

I would later find out through DNA testing that a branch of my father's family originated in Senegal and Guinea-Bissau. My mother's family originated in Nigeria and Cameroon. Liberia was not ancestral in a precise sense but it felt every bit like home in terms of the people and the culture. The Liberians I met looked me right in the eyes, square in the face. They really, really wanted to connect. They wanted to touch us. They held our hands when they talked. They hugged. They'd lock arms to walk together.

In every place we visited, before we got there we could hear the drums or women ululating in the distance. There was a lot of ceremonial dancing. I've always loved dancing and felt at home joining in. At one of our stops we were escorted to a river bank on a long path. The men walked ahead and the women followed, dancing and singing as they went. The rhythm was like nothing I'd heard, but I felt like I knew it and fell right into the beat, moving in step with the Liberians.

Everywhere felt to me like sacred ground, especially after watching a play our hosts put on for us that was a reenactment of the slave trade. It's one thing to look at a reproduction of slave quarters on a restored and landscaped plantation in Maryland. It's quite something else to watch Africans acting out their history at the very place where those slaves had been shackled and whipped as they boarded the ships that took them to places like Maryland. It made their history come alive and it made their history mine as well.

Made in the USA
Middletown, DE
26 June 2017